LEADERSHIP
DEVELOPMENT AND PRACTICE
A Biblical Perspective

LEADERSHIP
DEVELOPMENT AND PRACTICE
A Biblical Perspective

Samuel Mathew

2013

Leadership Development and Practice: A Biblical Perspective
—Published by the Rev. Dr. Ashish Amos of the Indian Society for Promoting Christian Knowledge (ISPCK), Post Box 1585, 1654, Madarsa Road, Kashmere Gate, Delhi-110006.

© Author, 2013

All rights reserved. No part of this book may be reproduced or transmitted in any form or by any means, electronic, mechanical, photocopying, recording, or by any information storage and retrieval system, without the prior permission in writing from the publisher.

The views expressed in the book are those of the author and the publisher takes no responsibility for any of the statements.

ISBN: 978-81-8465-298-7

Laser typeset by
ISPCK, Post Box 1585, 1654, Madarsa Road, Kashmere Gate, Delhi-110006
• *Tel:* 23866323/22
e-mail: ashish@ispck.org.in • ella@ispck.org.in
website: www.ispck.org.in

Contents

Foreword ... vii

Preface ... ix

Chapter 1
Leadership: Honourable Ambition ... 1

Chapter 2
Leadership and Development:
Biblical Foundations ... 13

Chapter 3
Servant Songs: Reflections on Qualities and
Characteristics of Servant-Hood ... 49

Chapter 4
Pauline Insights into Leadership: Imitate Me ... 77

Chapter 5
Leadership for Tomorrow ... 101

A Prayer ... 123

Bibliography ... 124

Foreword

While following older and existing leaders, young and emerging leaders usually confront a lot of confusion and many problems. It is therefore advisable to look at Scriptural values and norms related to leadership. This book written by my old friend and a dear brother in the Lord sheds significant light on leadership—especially leadership in the Church.

The author has elaborately and constructively discussed leadership development based on the Old and New Testaments. Leaders in the Old Testament times readily gave their lives for their people; they had the mindset of the Lord himself. Jesus, who fulfilled as an absolutely obedient servant the service God has expected and required of the people of Israel, is the call and requirement upon each Christian to be advocates of such invaluable qualities in their daily lives. The exemplary life and leadership of the apostle Paul have laid a solid foundation for leadership training and development. The role and service of a pastor are indisputably crucial for the emergence and development of a leader. An intimate relationship with the Holy Spirit is cited as a key to leadership development—something that this book highlights. The chapter on "leader of tomorrow" provides ice-breaking and challenging perspectives for young and emerging leaders. In my view, there is no other book that has been written in recent times with such an understanding of the Scriptures and biblical insights into leadership.

In this book, the author has adequately demonstrated the practicality and authenticity of his assumptions while bringing into sharp focus an array of scholars and leaders who are presently involved in leadership development.

Guidance for upcoming leaders, exemplary leader-behaviour, leadership style, attitude towards co-leaders—these are some of the subjects so passionately discussed in this book. In an interesting manner, the author not only presents a leadership model that is appropriate for the Indian Church but also gives a holistic and balanced perspective on leadership. This work is a wonderful guidebook to leadership development, especially Christian leadership; and it will surely instill a deeper commitment in the reader to become a leader in order to serve God and humanity in the best way possible.

Dr. George Samuel
Navajeevodayam, Tiruvalla, Kerala

Preface

Why another book on leadership? This book is special because it tries to renew our view on leadership from God's point of view. Based on God's word, it a guidebook for those who are aspiring to stand up for the Lord and his people by becoming capable leaders. In other words, this book, which is an expanded and revised version of my book in Malayalam titled, *Leadership Models* (Nethrutha Mathruka), focuses on what the Bible says about leadership and delegation and gives valuable insights into leadership development in the Church. Young and emerging church leaders and those who are intending to become a part of church leadership will find this book highly useful.

By and large, there has always been a crisis of leadership in our country, particularly within the Church. The Church in India, which is currently suffering a severe crisis of leadership, needs leaders who can lead her in the twenty-first century. Not many are committed to the task of grooming and developing the Church to stand and face her crises and challenges. In today's scenario, analysing Christian leadership from the biblical perspective and developing a renewed vision of church leadership are of paramount importance. This book promotes the Christ-like leadership pattern of "not to be served but to serve" and looks into the importance of formulating a relevant leadership pattern for today's Church.

Chapter 1

Leadership: Honourable Ambition

People around the world are searching for leaders—leaders whom they can follow in truth and reality. Concern about having a leader who is competent and gifted in meeting the needs of society, family units, organisations, churches and individuals is a common cry of our time and day. The search for efficient and effective leaders continues. It is no overstatement to say that the world is divided into leaders and followers.[1] A Christian leader is, nevertheless, involved in a very complex situation.

The success of any organisation, industry, institution, church or family depends largely on the kind of leadership it possesses. The growing need for effective leadership is increasingly felt today in the growing and challenging situation of the Church and our society. And growth itself, to a large extent, depends also on leadership capacities and endowments. It is undisputedly true that there is a leadership crisis in the Church today. It may be because of the leaders themselves, the life or organisation of the Church, or the particular leadership models, methods, styles and strategies employed. Whatever the reasons may be, the Church worldwide—particularly in India—is on the quest for revitalised and re-emphasised leadership.

It is the duty of the faith community to realise the truth that God is looking for people who will fill the gap and stand firm to lead the faithful in a world full of challenges, such as increasing population, turmoil, poverty, unjust exploitation of people and environment, oppression and the increasing emergence of capitalistic and imperialistic tendencies, alarming moral and ethical decline, and so on. "God is frequently represented as searching for a person of a certain type. Not people, but a person. Not a group, but an individual."[2] Many references from the Scripture suggest this idea, such as 1 Samuel 13:14, Jeremiah 4:25 and Ezekiel 22:30, which says, "And I sought for a man among them who should build up the wall and stand in the breach before me for the land that I should not destroy it; but I found none."

As told by a great saint of the yester years, a person whose faith is master of his mind to become a blessing to humanity, whose tongue is touched with heaven's flame to enlighten the people of all walks of life, a mighty prophet of the land to condemn injustice and unrighteousness and thereby bring justice and peace to earth—this is the kind of leader God is looking for to fill the gap and serve the purpose of His people. Ultimately, it is God alone who enables one to be an effective and charismatic leader.

Generally speaking, there has always been a leadership crisis, particularly within the Church. It is due to varied reasons, such as cultural, organisational and individual factors and complexities. We will raise a few of these issues in our study and attempt to find biblical answers to at least some of them.

The Church in India is in need of leaders who will provide vital leadership lead in the twenty-first century. It has very few who are effective; it finds not many who are committed to the task of grooming and developing the Church to stand and face its crises and challenges. The reasons for this are varied and many. In such a scenario, analysing today's Christian leadership from the biblical and theological perspective and imbibing a renewed vision are significant. By so doing, we shall attempt to analyse and evaluate the existing patterns of leadership in the Church on the basis of biblical revelations and understanding of servant-leadership. While keeping in mind the Christ-like leadership pattern of "not to be served but to serve", we will look into the importance of formulating a relevant leadership pattern for the Church today. Therefore, this book is fundamentally founded on the biblical theology of leadership.

An essential question to ask is who should be a leader. Should a person be ordained in order to obtain recognised leadership positions? What kind of strategy and model can we apply to leadership situations in India today? Is authoritarianism a well-defined and appropriate style or is it a servant lifestyle or team approach or a matrix structure? What kind of power and level of authority do and should we exercise? Is leadership merely an exercise of delegated power upon us by a structure or an organisation? Or can we define and restructure biblically based power and authority to include and embrace culturally injected and defined norms and the people finding fulfilment for their contributions as well?

Is servant-hood an appropriate model and concept of leadership, particularly in the context of India? Has a servant any authority? Can we redefine the concept of authority and power for our context and the changing scenario in India today? What are the basic models and patterns found in the Bible on leadership and, more particularly, on *spiritual* leadership? Was Jesus a servant-leader? Do we have such examples in our culture? Are we mistaken and moving away from the basics of biblical revelation when we consider insights into culturally-defined models of leadership, such as Mahatma Gandhi, contemporary *Gurus* who perform a teacher-disciple role, the Ashram movements and so on? Is it possible for one to incorporate biblical patterns of leadership into the already existing styles and norms of leadership in order to adequately communicate and build onto them a structure of relevant leadership?

Another issue that deserves consideration is the emergence of leaders. Who are the future leaders? Is there a vacuum in leadership today? Is hereditary succession normative to leadership emergence? If yes, what are its signs, and if not, what are the solutions? The issue of the old and elderly dominating the arena of leadership is yet another issue worth mentioning. How far is young leadership encouraged in the Church and society today? It is important to underscore the fact that one of the serious leadership crises that the Church and society face today in India is the wide gap between the older and emerging leaders. There seems to be a lack of open and sincere appreciation of the abilities and vigour of young leaders. In the same way, there is lack of planning and interest in providing proper contexts for the emergence and development of a future generation of leaders and in leading them to influential leadership spheres.

How do we evolve an adequate model and pattern for greater effectiveness in leadership without disregarding the culturally defined leadership concepts and biblically revealed servant-hood model? It is my genuine observation and feeling that these and many more issues, challenges and problems must receive serious and sincere consideration among many others.

This, then, will help promote greater effectiveness and growth of the Church and society and at the same time do justice to the word of God, the need and challenges faced and the context.

What Is Leadership?

Leadership is defined in many ways. It is usually attributed to leader-behaviour in directing a group towards a shared goal. Theorists give workable definitions of leadership according to their perspectives. We may not focus on one absolute definition in this regard. So, we will look at the various definitions given by different theorists and writers and try to combine the best features of these definitions to arrive at a comprehensive and workable definition.

If we are to define leadership in one single word, the word would be "influence." Leaders lead someone to the degree they influence others. The late President of America Harry Truman referred to leaders as "people who can get others to do what they don't want to do, and make them like doing it." Ted E. Engstrom defines a leader as follows:

> When I use the term leader in this book, I see him as one who guides and develops the activities of others and seeks to provide continual training and direction. This includes the president, administrator, executive, pastor, director, superintendent, superior department head, and so on.[3]

J. Oswald Sander states:

> Leadership is the capacity and will to rally men and women to a common purpose, and the character which inspires confidence... We are leaders to the extent that we inspire others to follow us.[4]

Robert Clinton deals competently with a number of issues in regard to leadership selection and development. According to him, leadership is,

> ...a dynamic process over an extended period of time in which a leader utilizing leadership resources and by specific

behaviours, influences the thought and activities of followers, toward accomplishment of aims—usually mutually beneficial for leaders, followers, and the macro-context of which they are a part.[5]

Clinton's definition of leaders is noteworthy. A leader is "...a person with God-given capacity and God-given responsibility who influences a group of followers toward God's purposes for the group."[6] Leadership is a complex task in a complex macro-context. It is not purely managerial skills and success. "A leader is a man who knows the road, who can keep ahead, and who pulls others after him."[7] Reverend P. T. Chandapilla, one of the late student leaders of our nation, defined leadership as a vocation where there is a perfect blending of both human and divine qualities and a harmonious working of God and persons.[8] It would be proper to note the differences made by Olan Handrix between leadership and management as quoted by Engstrom in his book as follows:

> Leadership is a quality; management is a science and an art. Leadership provides vision; management provides realistic perspectives. Leadership deals with concepts; management relates to functions. Leadership exercises faith; management has to do with fact. Leadership seeks for effectiveness; management strives for efficiency. Leadership is an influence for good among potential resources; management is the coordination of available resources organised for maximum accomplishment. Leadership provides direction; management is concerned about control. Leadership thrives on finding opportunities; management succeeds on accomplishment.[9]

Christian leaders are those who know that theirs is a ministry reflecting the supreme Leader, the Minister—Jesus Christ himself—and that they are a continuation of what is initiated by Him. Leaders are people-oriented and are to be people-persons. They represent a group of people with rights and various tastes; they attempt to honour those diversities. Christian leaders are those who look to Jesus as the model; for he said, "If anyone would be first, must be last of all and servant of all" (Mark 9:35). Therefore, they take leadership as a service and not as a position. Leadership operates between two poles: people on the one hand, and their goals, on the other. Leadership is the function of helping that body of people towards achieving their goals. The leader functions best as a trusted friend, and the prime means of leadership are the word of God and personal example. A good leader does not tell people that he or she has authority. A good leader has authority on his or her side, but he or she is not authoritarian. The most valuable guide for leaders to understand fellow human beings is to have a proper understanding of them first.

This is one of the noblest services. Leaders need to recognise their vocation as a ministry to serve people and God. Leadership in the Bible is viewed, first of all, as the influence the good one has on another. Christian leadership differs very much from political, secular and business leadership spheres. It differs in terms of its source, purpose, status, leader-follower situation and so on. A spiritual leader is the one who submits to the power and authority of the Sovereign God. Jesus made it very clear to the disciples on many occasions during his life and ministry. "It shall not be so among you; but whoever would be great among you must be your servant, and whoever would be first among you must be your slave..." (Matt. 20:26, 27). Leadership is, therefore, a kind of service. Leadership is a leader-act of influencing a group or person with a blending of both natural and divinely endowed capacities, authority, holistically and divinely shaped behavioural styles towards accomplishing God-given objectives, plans and purposes for and of a group, church and organisation through interpersonal influence and specifically given power in a given situation. This includes elements such as leader, follower and organisational and immediate situations. He or she is a servant-leader.

Joe S. Ellis aptly concludes what has been discussed so far:

> In some ways it is easier to be an authoritarian than a servant leader. The latter requires more skill, greater discipline of attitude and behaviour and clearer understanding of the task than the former does. But servants are far greater. Now the gentile idea of greatness is inverted, turned upside down, the pyramid resting on its apex, the great person bearing the lesser person on his back. The highest emblem of Christian leadership is not the whip of the lion tamer, but the towel and basin. The lion tamer stance is not nearly as effective in dealing with people as is the humble servant. The great leader portrays the Christ who sacrifices his all for his people.[10]

Therefore, Christian leadership is committed to people reflecting the model of Jesus' leadership pattern and development.

The questions raised above, among a host of others, highlight the need for careful thinking on leadership in our day. This book is based on the Holy Bible, written materials on the subject, reflections on personal experiences, and interactions and dialogue with various leaders and people at different times. It may have, therefore, its own limitations. Obviously, the issues raised and those before us are too large and challenging to be discussed in a small book like this one. Nevertheless, we will try to arrive at satisfactory solutions, conclusions and reconciliations by adopting biblical and theological perspectives. The book also looks for definite missiological and ministerial applications that are appropriate and relevant to the Church and the Indian context.

The objectives of this book are as follows:

- To explain thoroughly and bring a holistic understanding of the foundations of leadership in the Bible.

- To underscore the leadership of Jesus Christ in order for developing a Christ-like leadership in our situations.

- To make a brief study of selected passages from the writings of Paul and delineate Pauline thoughts on leadership and development.

- Gleanings on the "servant songs" and reflect the qualities and characteristics of a servant.

- To analyse how far the biblically defined servant character is ideal for any leadership situation in the Indian context.

- To analyse prevalent leadership patterns and norms in the light of biblical understanding of leadership and draw suggestions and recommendations for the future.

- To evolve a relevant pattern of leadership for the Church and public services.

Honourable Ambition

"Here is a trustworthy saying: If anyone sets his heart on being an overseer, he desires a noble task" (1 Tim. 3: 1). This was the exhortation of the Apostle Paul while writing to young Timothy, the emerging leader of the Church. Why is there dearth of able, skilled, fruitful, qualitative and effective leaders in our time? One of the early days' experiences and setting of my life would be a motivation and guide to us here in this regard.

On a beautiful evening in August 1977, four of us in a mission team were engaged in a conversation. We were worn out and tired after an exhaustive day's work; and we were actually sharing, praising God for what He had done on that day and praying for those with whom we had been connected in sharing the love of Jesus Christ. Unexpectedly, the leader of the team beckoned me to meet him in the office. Our State leader of the mission was also present there.

"Brother Samuel, I have called to tell you that you have been selected as the leader for this team" he whispered. The State leader affirmed, "Since your present team leader has been moved to another place, you need to lead this team." I just could not believe my ears! I had not even dreamt of "leading" a team.

Sir, "I do not think in any way that I can do it" I responded. "We, for some time, have been praying to the Lord to raise a person for the team and the mission station. And we are confident that God desires to entrust that responsibility to you. Let us not forget that God does not just look for those who are able and skilled, but for those who are committed, loyal and faithful and have surrendered their lives fully to Him." The leader pronounced these statements and then prayed with me.

There was within me not even a small degree of desire to be a leader. I was just a shy, unskilled person. But I had been brought to that place to believe that the Lord was calling me to that leadership. I submitted and surrendered myself as I knew that the Lord had entrusted the responsibility to me. It was only the beginning of the Lord's trust upon me for great and awesome responsibilities thereafter. The Lord had taught me all along the journey since then that leadership was not selection or appointment of a human being but an overwhelming call and an honorable ambition. It calls also for a fair amount of self-sacrifice, suffering and struggle.

God calls a person with a definite purpose. I have slowly learned that when he calls, he also endows and empowers. We must not say "no" to God's call. A call to lead and involve in any activity of worth should not be given up by making meagre excuses. We should learn to submit ourselves to experiencing the empowering and sustaining presence of God Almighty that makes us strong in our weakness. In the years that followed, the Lord was pleased to trust me with varied responsibilities for training, equipping and leading the people of God. The Lord had instructed that the call to leadership was a great call to a greater ministry and deeper learning.

What are the causes of the dearth of leadership in our Christian world? First, it is the ignorance and lack of faith in our capabilities and capacities. Instead of faith and optimism, we entertain negative thoughts, such as 'I have just one talent and so nothing can be done with it.' 'I can do nothing' is the attitude we relish. Second, some are fearful to employ their gifts and talents. I have heard many say, 'O had I got an opportunity to speak at that meeting, that convention, that place... Had I been placed in that position... that vocation or job...that responsibility...!' But when the opportunity comes by, they are unwilling to commit; rather they shy away making lots of excuses. We become as though paralysed, seeing the 'cants' than the 'cans.' Third, it is lack of vision. We cannot accomplish anything without possessing a long-term, large and big-enough vision, wholesome perspectives, positive thinking and optimism, divine guidance and innovations. Fourth, it is sheer lack of preparation and training—the equipping. This is a huge impediment. Some say, now I am not ready for any training; I will do it later. Yet others say 'I am too old for any kind of training'; 'I am no more able to learn anything now as before.' Fifth, it is the unwillingness to pay the price in and for leadership. An attitude of self-sacrifice and sincere endowments are extremely important and called for in the mission of leadership. For many, it is so difficult, particularly for young emerging leaders.

Why yet another book on this subject that is one subject among all the others so vastly discussed and written? After all, there exist many practically relevant books in this one area.

What is a new message we find in this book? The only way I can try to appease that query is by saying this. It is a gentle attempt to bring about a refocus, renewal, revamping of perspective and practice on the most foundational characteristics, nature and principles of leadership theory and practice from God's point of view—a Biblical mandate for all who are in and aspiring into any kind of leadership.

Further, this book is written not because the author has achieved or is perfect in all these invaluable virtues and lessons on leadership. I am humbled when doing it, and am a servant of God standing in the same place requiring grace and mercy as any one else trying to learn and become. But have attempted to put these in a book form for being a helping tool to all who desires the best in life for God and humanity. This book then is a journey in this process and quest. It will assist lead us to fulfillment of this beautiful aspiration within us and become God-ordained in our leadership pursuit.

Endnotes

[1] Ted E. Engstrom, *The Making of a Christian Leader,* Grand Rapids: Zondervan Publishing House, 1976, p.15.

[2] J. Oswald Sanders, *Spiritual Leadership,* Chicago: Moody Press, 1980, p. 18.

[3] Engstrom, *op.cit.*

[4] Sanders, *op. cit.*, p. 31, 33.

[5] Robert J. Clinton, *The Making of a Leader,* Colorado Springs: Navpress, 1988, p. 14, 245.

[6] *Ibid.,* p. 21.

[7] Sanders, *op.cit,* p. 32.

[8] P. T. Chandapilla, *Leadership,* Unpublished article for private circulation among student workers.

[9] Engstrom, *op. cit,* p. 23.

[10] Joe S. Ellis, *The Church on Purpose—Key to Effective Church Leadership,* Ohio: Standard Publishing, 1982, p. 132.

Chapter 2

Leadership and Development: Biblical Foundations

Leadership and development are a day-to-day intervention of God, which involves developing people for His purpose. Clinton writes, "When Christ calls leaders to Christian ministry, He intends to develop them to their full potential. Each of us in leadership is responsible to continue developing in accordance with God's processing all of our lives."[1] Nonetheless, a leader cannot suddenly become a perfect leader and influence a group in a perfect manner. Leadership is a lifetime of God's lessons, and each lesson and situation will be unique for each leader. God will take a leader or person of his choice through many leadership developmental processes or stages on his or her way to a lifetime of service.[2]

Our study in this chapter will be strictly limited to biblical and theological perspectives and foundations as found in this process and briefly discuss each of them. We will particularly look into the following areas in this study:

- The Old Testament and New Testament Patterns for Leadership Development

- The Role of a Pastor in Leadership Development
- The Role of the Holy Spirit in Leadership Development

Clinton defines development as "...a measure of a leader's changing capacity to influence in terms of various factors over a time; it is also used to indicate the actual patterns, processes, and principles that summarize development."[3] The task of training church leadership is, therefore, a vital aspect of the mission mandate. Therefore effective leaders recognise leadership selection and development as a priority function. "Effective leaders increasingly perceive their ministries in terms of a lifetime perspective."[4]

Leadership Formation and Development

Gleanings from the Old Testament

In this section, we will focus on two aspects: (1) the call and (2) training, formation and development. It will be based on gleanings from the Old Testament passages.

The Call

The first step towards developing strong and sustainable leadership comes through the divine call. "The divine call was never absent from the life experiences of Old Testament leaders."[5] This is so clearly seen as we take note of the prominent leaders of the Old Testament. The Scripture shows that the Holy Spirit inspired the writers to make mention of the call of priests, prophets, kings and such leaders at the very beginning of their vocation itself. For example, Moses (Exod. 3:7-10), Gideon (Judges 6:11-18), Amos, Jeremiah, Isaiah and Ezekiel (Amos 7:14-15; Jer. 1:1-10; 1 Sam. 6:1-9; Ezek. 2:1-10). In the New Testament, we find the disciples of Jesus and the Apostle Paul (Acts 9:15-16). There are many other giants in history, such as Martin Luther, John Wesley, William Carey, Hudson Taylor and so on. It is worthwhile to note here that "not all Christian leadership theorists agree with the concept of a call."[6] Sanders says:

> Both Scripture and the history of Israel and the Church attest that when God does discover a man who conforms to His spiritual requirements, who is willing to pay the full price of discipleship, He uses him to the limit despite his patent shortcoming. Such men were Moses, Gideon, David and a host of others.[7]

Sheldon Blank describes four common characteristics of a prophetic call: a conviction of mission, a feeling of inadequacy, a ministry of communication and a consciousness of the magnitude of the task.[8] Johannes Lindblom is also noticeable in this aspect. He says:

> The legitimacy of the true prophet and the authority of his message are established by his call. He knew that he was properly called by Yahweh to carry out his task. The false prophet is declared to be such as his visions and messages are rejected as valueless not because he did not have visions and ecstatic experiences, but because he had not been called.[9]

The coming of "the word of the Lord" (*dabur*) seems to be an integral part of the call in the lives of the prophets of the Old Testament. It is explicitly reflected in the expression, "Thus says the Lord." Yahweh spoke or imparted the Word to them, which eventually became the core of the prophets' communication. It is divine communication from God to the prophet and the prophet to the masses. The call of Yahweh determined this channel. David Watson writes, "A prophet must above all learn to listen to God, discern the voice of God, and then to pass on that word from God to his people."[10] It was the call that assured this divine "word" to them.

God is not interested in outward qualifications as humans are, for He looks upon the heart and desires that one should respond to the call and give oneself totally to him. Moses had set forth many excuses, but he was not really disqualifying. It was more in the sense that he was trying to get out of what God wanted him to do. Also, not because of recognising his inability or acknowledging God was able to do it.

The divine call can be summarised as follows: God always took the initiative, and the word came to the chosen one; the personal response of the acceptance to the call, although some refused. All ministries are God's ministry. Jesus introduced or set the pattern of our ministry when He said, "My food is to do the will of my Father that sent me." The development of leadership begins when the call of God comes and when we submit to obey that call.

Training and Development of Leaders

As we think about leadership and development, we also cannot push aside the truth that certain preparations take place in the lives of leaders even before they are called of God. God sees persons as they are and always accepts their natural abilities. In the process, He will purify, modify and strengthen humans to achieve His purposes. When God calls a person to a divine task, he also equips that person for the task. This principle has strong biblical support. "This divine enabling is possible before or after the call."[11]

Development includes all of life's processes, not just formal training context. Leaders are shaped by deliberate training and varied experiences. "Leadership development" is a much broader term than leadership training. Leadership training refers to a thin part of the overall process focusing primarily on learning skills. Leadership development includes this, but much more.[12]

The distinction between training and development must clearly be established and understood. 'Training' may refer to a limited period of formal learning; whereas 'development' is not limited to a particular time, space or training; it is a lifelong process. We are being developed each time when a lesson is appropriated into life. Therefore, learning is a lifelong process of lessons directed to development in every aspect. In the broad arena of leadership development, we will examine a few selected aspects of leadership training as it relates to leadership development.

Direct Personal Encounter with God

In the Old Testament, we observe many situations when God directly confronts in developing leadership of his chosen ones. God encounters them not only by speaking to them, but also by demonstrating his mighty power through various miracles to strengthen their faith. He also makes a clear promise to be with them. The leadership development of each of them was carried out through countless personal struggles and sour experiences; and this continued all through their lives and ministries. Such were people like Moses, Abraham, Joseph, Joshua, David, Jeremiah and so on. God has developed these persons even through failures in life. This produced character, deeper and greater trust and diligence in their leadership.

Consider the forty long years Moses had to spend in the wilderness and the equal span of time in the palace. This period of development was both formal and informal in nature. The leadership preparation of Joseph sheds great spiritual truths and insights applicable to all. He became a strong, stable and outstanding leader whose skills were recognised by all because of his faithfulness to God through many years of hard, painful and yet indispensable time of formation, training and equipping. He is a proof to the fact that a person can remain true to God and his or her vocation even in the midst of adversities and temptations. This has much similarity to the lives of the kings and the prophets of the Bible as well. Francis A. Schaeffer uses Joshua as an example of God's direct encounter in developing leadership, which could be an appropriate concluding statement here.

> After all the years of preparation, Joshua was now marked, in the presence of God's people, as the man of God's choice. Thus he would have learned that leadership, if it is real, is not from men. It was not even from Moses but only from God. Men can ordain, but leadership generated by men is only on the level of any human leadership and will bring no more spiritual results than any human charisma.[13]

Institutional Training

The people of Israel were a group of well-informed and educated people. Their training was primarily through their parents, religious leaders or priest, scribes and prophets. It was centred on the laws of God. Religious, moral and ethical and historical goals were linked together in the training (Exod.10:2; Deut. 4:9, 10, 6:7-9, 33:10).

Family

The primary education centre was the home and it centred on the parents. The mother was to teach the rudiments of character formation and it focused on moral formation (Prov. 1:8; Ps. 119:9-11; Prov. 22:6, 6:20, 31). One of the most sacred duties of the father was to train his son in the religious precepts (Exod. 10:2, 12:26, 13:8; Deut. 4:9, 6:7, 20). Thus the religious, moral and ethical aspects of a person's development were to be carried out at home. It was the Lord's command to the parents to teach their children to love the Law of the Lord with all of their hearts. There is no mention of schools for children other than this in the Old Testament. Deuteronomy 4:9, 10 projects the purpose of education:

> Only take heed, and keep your soul diligently, lest you forget the things which your eyes have seen, and lest they depart from your heart all the days of your life; make them known to your children and your children's children—how on the day that you stood before the Lord your God at Horeb, the Lord said to

me, 'Gather the people to me, that I may let them hear my words, so that they may learn to fear me all the days that they live upon the earth, and that they may teach their children so (Deuteronomy 4:9, 10).

Religious Institutions

The sanctuary was not only a place of worship and service of the priests but also a centre of training for them. Samuel is accepted among biblical scholars as a transitional leader between theocracy and monarchy. He received the call from the Lord and instruction from Eli while in the temple. The prophet Isaiah received his call while in the temple. There, he was further educated and trained to see himself—his true nature, his God—in utter holiness, and then the need around—as the people's spokesperson for God (Isaiah 6).

Samuel began his training for the priesthood as a child (1 Sam. 1:18, 28) by ministering to the Lord before Eli, the priest in the temple at Shiloh (3:1). He should have been watching over the sanctuary, for it says in the Word that "Samuel was lying down within the temple of the Lord" (3:3). His duty also included opening and closing the doors of the sanctuary early in the morning (3:15). Thus the training was partly being a temple-servant. Notwithstanding, Samuel's training was far from ideal due to the undiscerning character of Eli and the wickedness of his sons (1Sam. 2:12,17; 3:13; 2:29).[14] Samuel's training was an apprenticeship, both informal and in-service, a model advocated by certain proponents of leadership theories. The Sanctuary was the place where the priests were to teach, read and instruct the people of Israel in the Torah (Deut. 33:10).

Later in Israel's history there arose prophetic guilds. Prophets had a distinctive role in the leadership and development of the Israelites. There was also a school of prophets at the time of Elijah (1Kings 18:4, 13, 19:18). Scholars have pictured the ecstatic nature of these bands by stating that ecstasy was the distinctive feature of early prophets. There is mention of a company of prophets in 1 Samuel 19:20ff, when David flees and wandered from King Saul. Edward J. Young rightly says, "We are probably not far wrong if we assume that it was Samuel whom God used in the establishment of these bodies."[15] We also acknowledge that, in addition to the "sons of the Prophets", which appeared at the time of Elijah and Elisha (1 Kings 20:35; 2 Kings 2:3, 4:1, 6:1), there is also mention of the disciples of Isaiah to whom he conveyed his message (1 Sam. 8:1, 16, 30:8). It is noteworthy that these guilds had educative, cultic and literary functions among the people of Israel. James Wood is correct when he says that these bands "...were probably training groups, men getting ready to become prophets as their life work, Samuel in his day and Elijah and Elisha in their day seem to have been their teachers."[16]

Interpersonal Tutors

Most leaders of the Old Testament times were shaped through daily life situations right from their childhood although individually they may not have recognised it themselves. Except for the priesthood, the leadership was not hereditary in the Old Testament. The leadership development models such as, apprenticeship, in-service, discipleship and informal training methods are advocated by the leadership field. The trainee learns from the life and character of his or her teacher. The saying, "learning is not only by hearing, but also by seeing and doing" fits very well here. Elijah and Elisha are good examples of this. They could be thought of as "guardians" or "rulers of the city" (2 Kings 10:1, 5-6) or "nurses" (2 Sam. 4:4).

The following statements by Francis Schaeffer on the preparation of Joshua for leadership rightly fit in here. These insights could also very well apply to leadership development in general.

God will not tolerate the rebellion of people against himself. Power is not merely the power of the general and the sword. It is not to be the power of human, but the true power is the power of God. God is not far off; God is always immediately present. Sin is terrible especially among the people of God. Merely using the name of God is not sufficient. God can and will guide. A person cannot bind God with human-made rules. Even in his judgement, God keeps his promises and distinguishes among people. He does not treat people like a series of numbers. God's glory must come first. There is a big difference between leadership and self-aggrandizement. A person of God must stand and trust God even against one's own people, whether he or she is in the minority or in the midst of physical danger. True spiritual leadership does not come from the hands of men, but from God. No man is indispensable, yet each one is important and unique. Usually there is preparation before leadership.[17]

A common feature so vividly noticeable in all of these leadership examples is the sacred or divine enabling each one of them received for their role. And the natural abilities were adequately combined with the divine endowments.

What does one say about the difference between leadership "training" and "development" in relation to the Old Testament records? The development of a leader was within the context of life and ministry situations. The family had tremendous role in the whole process. The community of faith, who recognised the potential, spearheaded and supported the emergence of an emerging leader. The model of discipling and apprenticeship in development was akin to the process. It took a long period for God to prepare leaders like Moses, Joshua, the judges, David and the many others. Can one limit oneself to a certain block of time, method, style and approach to leadership training and development? What would Moses have done if he were placed in an Indian situation? Would the same style have been the model taken by Joshua, Samuel, or the other prophets? These are aspects to think about and study further. However, there is an absolute divine and foundational principle for spiritual leadership that is applicable to any situation and every leader.

The following observations summarise the Old Testament data on leadership training and development:

- The training revolved around people who had a divine call to certain tasks, and the call did not preclude the necessity of training.
- Training was observed in various ways: formal, informal and non-formal; in which training models such as apprenticeship, discipling and in-service were prevalent.
- The trainers were parents and religious leaders, such as priests, scribes, prophetic guilds, etc. It was often or always in real-life situations.
- The training was obedience-oriented and content-oriented and had the strong element of memorisation and oral repetition.
- In training and development, natural abilities were equally considered with those of divine endowments.
- The trainee is given an opportunity to practice specific tasks in a controlled environment before he or she is actually placed into the profession.
- Very often both the trainer and the trainee had to find their development through difficult and adverse situation and intense pressure and opposition.

Gleanings from the New Testament

In the section above, we saw that the core elements in facilitating development were that of the family and the community of faith. It was an in-service and apprenticeship model with a view on a long-term process and in real life situations. Training was not limited to formal education; it began from early childhood itself.

In this section, we will study two outstanding and distinct personalities whose teachings are unique, and so, adequate enough for this study. First of all, based upon the Gospels, we will endeavour to understand the unique philosophy of Jesus. Secondly, with a broad outlook on the writings of Saint Paul, we will derive the philosophy and approach to leadership training and development. The Apostle Paul was a great leader the Church saw after Jesus Christ. He had pioneered and established churches in Asia and appointed leaders to oversee its growth and development. It will be an interesting study to observe and analyse a range of factors in training and development of leaders from these outstanding sources of information within the New Testament narratives.

Jesus' Pattern for Leadership Development

As a foundational thought, the home was the centre of education in the days of Jesus Christ. Although the synagogue had gained prominence in his day, the real centre of education continued to be the home.[18] One cannot hold an absolute view that formal schools existed during the days of Christ. However, few scholars hold this view and agree to the fact that the formal school system was in effect.

"Jesus' first teachers were his earthly parents."[19] The account of his adulthood is briefly yet emphatically narrated in the Lucan account: "And Jesus increased in wisdom and in stature, and in favour with God and man" (2:52).

In order to comprehend the training pattern of Jesus, terms such as "the twelve," "disciple," and "discipleship" require serious consideration. "Disciples" included a larger circle than the "twelve" (John 6:60, 66- 67). The original word *mathetai*, which means 'disciples', refers to anyone who faithfully follows Jesus Christ as Lord and is a responsible member of His Church.

Jesus is and was unique in his approach to training and developing future leaders. This uniqueness is nothing but the 'in-ministry' or 'in-service' method carried out by him in the process. It was a discipling model, so much so that it was a model of discipling in a regulated setting. It had the emphasis on a 'Rabbi-disciple' or 'teacher-student' relationship. Jesus must have adapted the existing model from the religious circle prevalent on that day. But this was certainly different in its quality and style. It was not merely passing on of knowledge and information as was found in the teaching of the rabbis of his day. It may not have been even a "guru-sishya" (teacher-disciple) model of the "holy men" of the present times who merely pass on the "ways-to-do" to the followers, but not so much so lived in.

Jesus and his group were itinerants who learned and received training while on the job. In this manner, Jesus was very unique in developing future leaders of his Kingdom. It may be that John the Baptist and his disciples were also itinerant evangelists. Truly so, but he never trained them for a long term as Jesus did, and his was a ministry for preparing the way of Jesus. Jesus is unique all the way; and none can be like him as far as Messiahship and the uniqueness of his person are concerned.

We conclude therefore, that unconditional call to discipleship, Rabbi-disciple relationship, active in-service discipling, a call to absolute loyalty and submission through all life situations were so prominent ingredients and uniqueness a style of Jesus our Lord. He demonstrated it to us through his own servant-hood leadership style and by investing in and developing his own disciples as well. We must follow him all the way.

Discovering the Style of Training

Foremost of all, Jesus took the *initiative*. He selected the disciples regardless of their personality, vocation and background. Jesus sent his disciples to *proclaiming* him rather than creating a school (Mark 6:7-13). It was *practice* rather than learning theories. Jesus called them to a total *allegiance* to himself. Being the true disciples of Christ, they were to be the leaders of the new and growing community—the Church. Christ gave preference to the *experiential* component in the training of his disciples. T. W. Manson in his writings convincingly relates the term "disciple" to the Aramaic *sewilya,* that is, "apprentice"; rather than to *talmid* meaning "student". He states:

> Discipleship as Jesus conceived it was not a theoretical discipline of this sort (referring to scribal system), but a practical task to which men were called to give themselves and all their energies. Their work was not study but practice... Jesus was their Master not so such as a teacher of right doctrine, but rather as the Master craftsman whom they were to follow and imitate. Discipleship was not matriculation in a Rabbinical College but apprenticeship to the work of the Kingdom.[20]

The word "follow" (*akoloutheo*) is a reference to Jesus' disciples or the followers of Jesus. To follow rather than to learn should be the true mark of a disciple of Christ. The three-fold ministry of the twelve as expressed by the gospel narrators are as follows:

- To be with him—making of a community
- To send them out to preach—making of heralds
- To have power over demons—the extension and continuation of His authority (Mark 3:14; John13:35)

Jesus appointed the twelve as apostles while yet undergoing his learning or training. The calling of the twelve was with an urgent missionary purpose (Matt. 10: 1, 2). This points towards the emphasis therein on the component of experience in training and development. Experience in ministry was an important part of Jesus' training programme for the twelve with the purpose of developing them as future leaders of the Kingdom. They were essentially "apprentices" who ministered while learning.

The Training

The three major concepts that ought to receive consideration concerning Jesus' training of the twelve are those of selection or call, the contextual factors and the methodology.

Selection (Call)

A divine call is the underlying basis of any leadership and ministry assignment. A note of caution should be mentioned here due to the consideration of both the selection and the call under the same heading. Both are divine work. The selection, however, is distinctly from God alone and could come at different stages in life as does also a call. The selection is only realised and recognised when individuals accept the call of God in their life. But the call is a greater impulse or inner-direction that comes to the lives of people (1Sam. 6:1-10; Jer. l: 4-19; Ezek. 2; Amos 7:14, 15; Acts. 13:2).

Jesus as the leader was concerned to train, equip and make these disciples devout, loyal and committed followers so that others could follow them. Coleman says, "Men were His method."[21] Jesus in training and developing his disciples *portioned* his life. Selection is an active element in leadership development. Elliston says, "The New Testament writers frequently use the word *'kaleo'* (call) and a related one was *'prokaleo'* (call to/toward). This 'calling' often indicates a selection or choice.[22] Selection or call is the confirmation to leadership or a ministry assignment. While people may train for leadership, only God calls."[23] Jesus, in developing and training his disciples, first of all called them and selected the few to activate the training process. This idea is inherent and vivid in the phrase "Follow Me." Jesus was concentrating on the few who could lead the multitudes. Coleman says:

> His only hope was to get people imbued with His life who would do it for Him. Hence, He concentrated Himself upon those who were to be the beginning of this leadership. Though He did what He could to help the multitudes, He had to devout Himself primarily to a few people, the selected few rather than the masses.[24]

In the process of training and developing the style of Jesus, he required that people decide where they want their ministry to count—in the momentary applause of popular recognition or in the reproduction of their lives in a few chosen men and women who will carry on the work. These may be people of humble status but people who are willing to learn. For such, only such few, investment is of great worth. John Kirkpatrick writes:

> All contemporary leadership selection and training programs regardless of whether their context is in the East or West, must have a study of life and servant-hood of Jesus of Nazareth as a fundamental component.[25]

Thus the selection is for those willing and committed people who will learn and walk on the trail of servant-hood, which is the life of the Master himself.

Scope and Context

The arena or scope of the training was Jesus' own ministry. The context was the first-century Palestine. This portrays a modelling that takes place in the context of daily life situations or the actual ministry itself. Alexander Hay has made a significant observation on this point:

> The disciples were called upon to do nothing that they did not see their teacher doing. They learned to evangelize by following Him, seeing Him doing the work, sharing with Him the fatigue on the road, the heat of the day, the unceasing toil, dangers, the hopes and disappointments, the mocking and the triumphs. It

was there they learned to preach, to seek the lost, to have compassion on the multitudes. They watched His walk with absolute obedience to the Father's will. They saw Him forego all material wealth and live a life of faith. They saw as He continually went apart to spend long hours, even whole nights in prayer... They saw Him in Gethsemane as He yielded to God's will and to the Cross. Finally, they saw Him in His Resurrection life. By His own truth, humility, patience, and love, trained them to be no sluggards and to seek not ease and luxury, but to pray and work, to sow by all waters and to wait patiently for the fruit. [26]

Jesus Himself demonstrated and expounded the lessons through his life and actions. A few of them are as follows: The miracle at Cana (John 2:1-10), the authority demonstrated at the cleansing of the temple (John 2:12-24), the dialogue with Nicodemus (John 3), the conversation with the Samaritan woman (John 4), the raising of Lazarus (John 11) and the lone times he spent in prayer. In regard to the context and method, Glasser says:

> Jesus changed both the training methods he used and the content of his instruction. One should draw from this the profound awareness that no one type of 'follow up' ministry or leadership training is normative for all situations. Methods must change because situations change and because spiritual growth itself makes new demands.[27]

Thus, the training of the disciples was involved in the context of ministry itself and they were to learn by doing.

Methodology

We must also consider the methodology of leadership training and development in this respect. This involves a very careful and intentional apprenticing of the disciples by Jesus. Maybe, it is good to view Jesus' methodology from both the 'pre-service' and 'in-service' training perspectives. The former refers to that which takes place prior to one's involvement in actual ministry and the latter to that which occurs in the context of the student's ministry formation.

However, the striking truth is that even while in a preservice training period, the followers were involved in ministry (John 4:2; Luke5:3; Mark 6:3ff); although the focus was on simple observation of Jesus' own ministry. Jesus' training method consisted of prayer, example and instruction.

The training objectives and leadership development could be found particularly in Luke 6:12-16 and Mark 3:13-19 and many other references in the Gospels, such as Mathew 28:18-20; 24:14; John 4:32, 5:30, 6:38, 8:28, 17:4. The appointment of the twelve was done after spending a night in prayer. In fact, this act of prayer was to become an essential component of Jesus' training method later on. Glasser writes:

> He was always the embodiment of what he sought to impart. For example, it was the reality of his prayer life that prompted his disciples to ask that he also teach them to pray (Luke 11:1). Their request confirmed to him that they were ready to receive his instruction... there is an underlying relation between Jesus' own prayers and his instruction on prayer.[28]

It was not until he had been with the disciples for more than a year, and upon their request, that Jesus gave them formal instruction on prayer, although he prayed frequently. We find that the basic method of our Lord was an example first, then precept; he continually set examples but instruction was infrequent or was only when they were perceived to be ready for it.

As mentioned before, their selection indicates two purposes: in-service discipleship and to send them out as preachers or custodians of the Gospel. Downey regards the first as the means whereby the second purpose was to be accomplished.[29] There is no doubt to the truth that both of these are intrinsically and intimately interrelated. From Jesus' perspective his goal was to share his life intimately with the disciples and to send them out as co-labourers in his ministry.

This is where personal sanctification of a leader is called for. In this, the leader is only fulfilling the interest of the Master and is interested in Him and not overwhelmed with personal interest but all margins of life are free and under the subjective, personal dominance of God alone.

The first purpose has an inference to the in-service methodology of leadership development. He chose them to be with him—to be companions, helpers, apprentices and followers during his active life and ministry while on earth. This was strongly an imitation model of training. Coleman rightly affirmed, "He did not ask anyone to do or be anything which first he had not demonstrated in his own life, thereby, not only proving its workability but also its relevance to his mission in life."[30] Their association with Christ and his ministry very much become a way of life (Mark 3:14, 15). It was both an emotional and an intellectual commitment for the disciples. Jesus purposed to share his life to the extent that they would be deeply effective on the job even after he was gone. It was achieved on-the-job by being itinerants and in-service apprentices. A very practical, down-to-earth, grass-roots approach and method that is very profound, yet taxing and resistible by many.

We have no right to judge where we should be put and to have preconceived notions as to what God is fitting us for. God engineers everything; wherever He puts us over and into, our great aim is to pour out a whole-hearted devotion to Him in that particular work. As it is said in the Scripture, "Whatever your hands finds to do, do it with your might." (Ecc. 9:10).

It was a call for a personal, dominant and solemn note of concentration on God—the Master, Leader. It is he who is important, the centre, the crux, the source of a leader and that is why this aspect is so relevant in leadership training and development. We should not worship our 'position,' 'leadership,' 'titles,' 'credentials' and 'the work'—it must be absorbed into the very essence and substance of the leader.

Considering this from the taxonomies of educational objectives, it is apparent that experiential, cognitive and effective taxonomies were integral parts of Jesus' training and development of the twelve.

Another dimension of Jesus' pattern was that of inculcation and formation of a lifestyle of preaching and exorcism. The plight of the disciples at the crucifixion of Jesus indicates that a mere telling of the truth is not sufficient in itself, but an actual experience in life is necessary. Many of the New Testament scholars observe that for the disciples the resurrection event itself was a significant teaching tool for a deeper understanding of the death and resurrection of Jesus. The cognitive domain is affected only when actual ministry experiences validate each of them. This is because of the inseparable relationship between the knowing, feeling, and doing dimensions of life. A leader of God's work must stand so much alone that one never knows that he is alone. Leaders must build faith, not on the feelings, things or people but on the Light that never fails or fades away, and stand sure for ever. It is worth reckoning that between the day of resurrection and Pentecost, the disciples went through a significant learning process. Alexander Balmain Bruce's statement clarifies this point:

> From the time of their being chosen, indeed, the twelve entered on a regular apprenticeship for the great office of apostleship, in the course of which they were to learn, in the privacy of an intimate daily fellowship with their Master, what they would be, do, believe, and teach, as "His witnesses and ambassadors to the world."[31]

One of the characteristics of good leadership is to prepare others to take over. The idea is not simply to "DO WELL," but to pattern oneself after the leader in every aspect—this is the norm. Not one of the twelve apostles was trained to become the

'Messiah' or the 'Son of God.' That is an absolute characteristic and the uniqueness of Jesus himself. Yet he handed over to us a great pattern or model for the ministry. Thus, it is ardently true to say that we are placed as representatives of our Lord, and in this regard, we need to reflect the very life of our Lord. Jesus worked towards this end by teaching, rebuking, training, building and showing them the way. This is the purpose of training others—to make leaders who will train others in order that they in turn may become leaders. Jesus started this by multiplying his physical capacity into twelve. This does not mean that he was multiplying his Messiahship, instead, his own aim, purpose, style, character—in other words, all of himself was poured into and passed on to the life of the disciples. This pattern of Christ in discipleship training is a solid foundation for leadership development.

Philosophy and Approach of Saint Paul

In the previous section, we derived patterns and methods from the life and teachings of Jesus Christ for leadership training, formation and development. It is good for us to now look into the Apostle Paul and bring into fore his life, teachings and writings in this regard. Paul, though not one among the twelve, has extensively served the cause of the kingdom of God. He had a unique style of handling the issues of leadership in the Church. He has not offered us a pattern of itinerants with three-and-a-half years of training as was of Jesus in developing any of his twelve disciples, except maybe to a few people like Timothy, Titus and Barnabas. The following discussion will shed further light on this point.

The writings of Paul have so much relevance to training, formation and development of leaders. Most of all, his writings are viewed and perceived primarily from the dogma of the Church than mere practice. And establishing correct doctrines, traditions and hierarchy seems to be the way most scholars approach the writings of Paul; and very rightly so, since we have no other biblical sources other than this apart from early traditions, history and saints. And so, the Church has got a philosophical, dogmatic and theoretical foundation in which alone a practice can be developed and validated.

Studying the book of Acts with a "leadership eye" will bring us close to recognising it as a resource book for leadership development in the early Church. Moreover, it establishes that the training of the twelve by Jesus is brought now to its perfection by the Holy Spirit himself. Through his wide range of writings, Paul has contributed to the history of the Church a wonderful leadership-development pattern.

The assumption that leaders tend to train others as they have been trained is highly significant. Jesus' saying that "...everyone after he has fully trained will be like his teacher" (Luke 6:40) has great significance in leadership training and development. Lawrence Richards says, "Part of the difficulty experienced by men moving into local church ministry grows out of the fact that example leadership does reproduce itself."[32]

A gleaning through the writings of Paul clearly underscores and establishes the principles of our Lord. Paul also employed the in-service, apprenticeship models used by his Master. And he deployed them with an absolute trust, upholding the dignity and personhood of individuals in developing young and emerging leadership for the Church and society.

Training Philosophy

The leadership trainees of Paul generally consisted of his companions, more specifically, the people who were designated to take up major roles in the ministry. Paul demonstrated great confidence by early appointment of the local church leadership. The book of Acts speaks of his appointment of leaders in local churches. He appointed them even before the end of his first missionary journey and return to Antioch. Rolland Allen emphasises the fact that elders were selected from among the local church members and that plural leadership rather than "one-man" leadership was the norm.[33] The noteworthy point is that the function of leadership is broader than filling an official position. Paul appointed leaders as soon as he established churches (1Thess. 5:12; 1Cor. 12:28). Dean S. Gilliland writes:

> Paul's priority was to find authentic resident leadership rather than postponing the appointment of elders while he, or one of the-apostolic team continue to govern, teach and control. But he did not abandon these newly-appointed leaders. He returned again and again to 'strengthen' these brothers as they hold the flock together.[34]

Apostle Paul left these leaders to develop leadership qualities on their own in the context of their in-service or actual ministry situations. This is one of the differences between Pauls' pattern of training and Jesus' pattern of training. The emergence of leadership was their own, though he had some role in selection (Acts 14:23). This is what we call a "laissez faire" attitude towards training.

Paul's philosophy of training was founded on the conviction that God is supreme in selection and development. The emphasis was on moral and internal skills rather than on academic qualities. The moral standards as a priority and prerequisite to training were as follows: A converted life, commitment to a redeemed community, personal ethics and morality above reproach and the filling of the Holy Spirit. For Paul, the best way to develop leaders was to encourage them to use the endowments of spiritual gifts that the Holy Spirit endows in order to build the community.[35]

Another salient feature of Paul's leadership development is the relationship he maintained with his companions and co-workers in the ministry. The theocratic structure and methodology of Paul for leadership development guaranteed an emergence of leaders at an early stage in the churches. Gilliland says, "We see five reasons why Paul had no second thought about an early, autonomous leadership for the churches.'

The reasons are listed below:
- Developing leaders at the early stage of a mission church fosters initiative..... Its growth, the quality of its witness and the administration of its life are not seen as the responsibility of an outsider but are accepted by the Church itself...
- It teaches equality. This stresses the distribution of gifts to all in the body and that all have opportunities for service (Rom. 12:5; 1 Cor. 12:28).
- Developing leaders at an early stage of a church encourages independence. Independence for each church and interdependence are in harmony with the gospel of freedom... Christians are to be trusted with responsibility...
- Developing leaders at an early stage promotes spiritual growth. Maturity is what Paul wanted most for his churches. It will help the leadership to find their own solutions and to work out their own problems. Growth enables function (ministry) and the function in turn promotes greater growth...
- Early leadership development emphasises contextual Christianity. It is the right to think and work out Christian life for themselves.[36]

Let us look at four important aspects of Paul's methodology. First, consideration should be given to the selection process. In choosing disciples, Paul's method was slightly different from that of Jesus. He depended on personal affirmation and recommendation of the local church. And with those selected colleagues, he genuinely, deeply and intimately shares his life for moulding and developing their leadership potentials, scope and skills.

Second, consideration should be given to his preaching and teaching method. The primary purpose of his preaching was to bring people to the living God and equip the believers for various ministries. His preaching was mainly to those who are not yet Christians. The book of Acts tells us that Paul stayed in Corinth, Ephesus and Rome for more than a year for preaching and teaching. He has been continually teaching those disciples and strengthening them in their faith (Acts 18:11; 19:8-10; 28:30, 31). Paul also visited them again for the same purpose. And, undoubtedly, in all these places, the apostle must have been involved in training the believers for church leadership. The letters of Paul to the churches testify to the fact that he had an ongoing plan for training and development for them in faith and leadership. The epistles discuss extensively the distribution of the gifts of the Holy Spirit and church leadership. This is the principal means of the expression of the kingdom of God and of the growth and development of the believers. His unselfish and intimate relationship with the elders of these churches was the fruit of his leadership training during his time of preaching and teaching.

The third aspect is in regard to pastoral commissioning. As his Master did, Paul also delegated the responsibilities to his disciples by sending them to pastor a local church. Such examples are seen in Timothy and Titus. They were fully authorised to organise the Church, to establish discipline and accountability and to promote the Christian cause. They were responsible for appointing overseers and elders.

The fourth aspect is training through writing. As we know, a major part of the New Testament belongs to the literary activities of Paul. This must be viewed primarily as a tool for leadership training and development. This was another unique pattern of Paul in training and development that is different from that of Jesus.

Paul concentrated on certain aspects of personality development and character formation of individuals as is evident in the letters to Titus and Timothy. He urges them to set a good example in life and deeds; in your teaching show integrity, gravity, speech that is beyond reproach, steadfast faith and purity. Attend to the public reading of the Scripture, to preaching and teaching. The ministry was to correlate with and correspond to their teaching and manner of life; otherwise, the influence and purity of their ministry would be nullified (cf. 1 Tim. 4:11-14).

Role of Pastor in Leadership Development

Leadership is not only the quality of a person but also an event in the life of a group. It is an expression of a "group." The Bible says that the Church is the body of Christ and that he is the Head of that living organism. The pastor is involved in bringing the whole family into maturity, in which all have a mutual, equal and disciplined part to play. He should reach that goal through 'group effort' or 'team play' rather than through an individual, arbitrary and authoritarian role. A genuine and godly pastor willingly and deliberately incorporates the believers of his church and their gifting into the total outworking of the life and ministry and creatively mobilises and motivates them into successful function. Otherwise, he is not a real and genuine pastor. Pastors must recognise and admit this to be necessary and normal for an efficient and effective function, development and growth of the Body. This function of the pastor is very well highlighted by Howard Snyder:

> In the community of God's people the pastor is not the head, the pastoral director, the boss or the chief executive officer, father the pastor (or better, pastors) serves as coordinator, equipper, discipler, overseer and shepherd. This is leadership. But it is leadership for, with, and in the body. It is leadership on an organic community model, not an organizational hierarchy model.[37]

The role of the pastor is crucial in the development and mobilisation of the Church as a whole and as a holistic community. His vision must be to disciple the members into leaders and mobilise the gifts of the members for the total and holistic outworking of the ministry. Leadership grows out of discipleship. Snyder says:

> The church has a shortage of 'ministers' only when it fails to see all believers as ministers and thus fails to disciple believers into leaders. A church that does not understand itself biblically puts low priority on discipling. It makes secondary qualifications for leadership primary and so with time inevitable runs short on leaders who are truly servants of the kingdom.[38]

It is legitimate to raise the following questions at this point: Which of the "gifts" are "leadership" gifts? Are all "followers" gifted? Do all followers of Jesus Christ have a role in the body, the Church? The Church is a living organism and all are as believer-priests having one or another functional role in the growth and development of the Church and its ministries. All of the 27 gifts mentioned in the Bible are equally important, not one less or higher than the other. It is the responsibility of the pastoral-leader to recognise, acknowledge and foster these gifts and lead the way being a catalyst providing a proper place of function and application in the Body for each gift. Each gift has its own application in its own place of function. However, one of the key functional purposes of a pastor-leader is to bring orderliness in the development of the Church collectively as a community and individually as members of the body. This is why the leadership of the Church is a function or role and not a position. The various gifts are for filling up the functions and not positions.

The leadership of the Church, therefore, is plural; and the foremost priority of the pastor is to disciple and develop men and women into leadership for the furtherance of the Kingdom. "The life and growth of the early church can be seen best as a community of spirit-filled Christians exercising their spiritual gifts."[39] A pastor should no longer be satisfied with an autocratic leadership style in the Church. A good pastor is one who will mobilise all the available resources among the members to the maximum growth and nurturing of the Body and for strengthening and enlarging the boundaries of scope and possibilities of leadership gifting. A pastor-leader should acknowledge and accept the eternal truth of the biblical vision that only a true Christian community becomes both the basis and goal of evangelism. The priority of equipping God's sheep or flock for 'kingdom living' and ministry should become the overall orientation, focus, vision and undergirding ethos of all pastoral functions. Peter Wagner writes, "Vital sign number one of a healthy church is a pastor who is a possibility thinker and whose dynamic leadership has been used to catalyst the entire church into action for growth."[40]

The pastor performs a dual function in leadership development in the Church, which are: teaching the Word and shepherding the flock. The purpose of teaching ministry is for developing the people of God into maturity—building them up into perfection. There should be, therefore, on-going programmes and activities in every local church designed for training and developing members. It is not different from discipling, for discipling is teaching (Matt. 28:18-19). Leadership is an important and decisive factor for church growth. This is "teaching them to observe all that I have commanded you" so that they also can be ministers. Thus, the Church as an organism will be equipped to avoid, solve and confront the unwanted problems and heresies; and eventually it will grow and multiply both qualitatively and quantitatively. This is why leadership development is crucial for the pastor of a local church. What is, therefore, the purpose of the pastor's teaching ministry in leadership development? One of the leading Christian educators, Kenneth O. Gangel, writes:

> The purpose of the church's education ministry is to make God's people mature so that they can minister. Maturity is an edification or a 'building up' process. Thus by education, the pastor can help his members to overcome frustrations and disappointments. And the church will be advanced to take more modest tasks, and demanding functions.[41]

As a catalyst, the pastor must provide the context for emergence and for doing the ministry in the process of leadership formation and development. This is crucial to grooming into maturity the young, vibrant, but childlike leadership potentials in the people. They are to encourage, support, equip, engage, prune and facilitate the followers to emerge as leaders and yet remain flexible. Elliston writes:

> The role of the existing leader then is to discern God's will, the emerging leader's condition and the situation to care for the new leader, his/her followers and the situation until the emerging "leader" can lead on her/his own... The existing leader may have to give more attention to the leader, the followers or the context to facilitate the process of development.[42]

Youssef states four progressive steps of leadership development that a pastor-leader should take into consideration: (1) People may not recognise their own leadership abilities until someone discovers them and gives them opportunities; (2) leadership emerges when people receive opportunities to develop themselves; (3) people emerge into leadership positions when they know they are wanted; and (4) most leaders learn on the job. This is the pastoral role for leadership development.[43]

The pastor is a guardian. If the pastor concentrates on developing more of the ministerial strength of the Church, the potential for its growth will be stronger. In developing leaders, the pastor helps them to discover and re-discover their spiritual gifts, teaches them to use those given gift(s) and motivates and inspires them with courage and conviction by being on the knees—the source of power. This is in order for the pastor-leader to set up goals for the congregation in guidance with the will of God by always looking ahead to accomplish them by and through total mobilisation of the Church and her gifts. The pastoral role reflects the work of the Holy Spirit. They give hands, feet, voice and face to the work of the Holy Spirit. Eddie Gibbs writes:

> Those who are in leadership positions do not merely exercise their gift on behalf of the congregation and with their official recognition; they are also responsible for stimulating those similarly gifted (but not necessarily with accomplishing leadership ability) in the congregation. In their ministries they will inspire others by their example and invite them to work alongside them. So the church becomes a 'gift-evoking' community.[44]

The pastor is a servant-leader in leadership development. He facilitates and identifies the contexts and opportunities and delegates ministry situations for the people of God. He needs to count at all times the cost of the job based on how he or she faithfully develops leaders for the ministry. The pastor can thus rejoice over his or her role by evaluating the efforts, energy and sacrifice poured into the development of leadership gifts for the advancement of God's kingdom on earth. He or she naturally does not endorse all gifts and charisma. A pastor's service is enhanced only when all the gifts in the Church are in operation and when they are carefully and faithfully utilised within the community. Snyder writes:

> This is the cost of servant-hood... . Because Christians are human, God-imaged persons—not sheep—pastoring goes beyond feeding and perfecting the flock to include transforming believers into priests, ministers, and servants in their own rights.[45]

Our churches, organisations, Bible seminaries and evangelistic endeavours will doubtlessly grow and bloom when we recognise and apply these fundamental principles. That is to say, the pastor or teacher—the existing leader—must have an unswerving commitment to providing, facilitating, selecting and praying with deep discernment of the Spirit and wisdom in guiding the young and gifted people in the community and using the gifts for equipping the body and its ministry.

Role of the Holy Spirit in Leadership Formation and Development

The Holy Spirit's role is crucial in leadership, as He is the guiding, stimulating, strengthening, empowering, loving, caring and imparting agent in the lives of leaders and matters of church growth. As the children of God and ministers of his Word, anything that is genuine and sustainable can only be produced and developed through the Holy Spirit. The real issue faced by leadership and development is our relationship with God the Holy Spirit.

The carnal nature of people, which is stubborn, selfish and rebellious, makes the Holy Spirit indispensable. This nature can be adequately transformed by the working of the Holy Spirit in the lives of individuals—the leader as the agent of the Spirit. Therefore, what Ronald W. Leigh has to say about the Holy Spirit's role is indisputable. He writes, "...the Holy Spirit supplies the spiritual dynamic for all Christian ministry. When the Holy Spirit is not active there can be no spiritual results in the ministry."[46] We cannot utter His words because we are without Holy words and can speak His holy words only when He rearranges, reconstructs and reconstitutes us.

The Spirit of God was an active agent both in the Old Testament and in the New Testament—in calling, separating, empowering and developing leaders. In the Old Testament, we see that the Spirit of the Lord moved from one leader to the next with anointing; so also, the fearful, less educated disciples of Jesus Christ became fiery mediums through the work of the Holy Spirit in their lifetime in the first century.

Accordingly, various functions and roles of the Holy Spirit can be underscored in connection with the leadership development of an individual and community. Some of them can be as follows: the Spirit calls, the Spirit gifts, the Spirit guides, the Spirit prunes, the Spirit moulds, the Spirit motivates, the Spirit unites, the Spirit enhances both the corporate and individual vision, the Spirit mobilises, the Spirit teaches, the Spirit brings conviction, the Spirit judges, and so on. In other words, the Spirit becomes and remains as the breath, water, dew and rain in enhancing and sustaining the atmosphere, contexts and development of every leader.

Above all, the Holy Spirit guides and leads the believers and the leader. The Spirit gives instructions and guidance to leaders that they themselves cannot. He indwells and captivates all of our being. The Spirit guides our ministry and ministries, especially in our conflicts, planning and decision making. The Spirit adds wisdom to our daily time table. The Spirit guides as to where we should go, what, how and when we should go (Acts 13: 1-4, 15:28, 29; Rom. 8:14, 26, 28). It is the Spirit who does this, so a leader in training and formation should acknowledge and be available and sensitive to the immutability of His involvement in life and making.

Another area worth considering is that the Spirit is the Giver of all spiritual gifts. It is noteworthy that Jesus himself has called out the presence of the Holy Spirit, saying that "the Spirit of the Lord has anointed me to preach the Good News to the poor." It is so vivid in the Gospel—that the Lord has been so dependent on the Holy Spirit to carry on the work the Father has given him. The dependence of the Lord demonstrates a commitment and eagerness for the Holy Spirit to fruition the abilities, scope, possibilities and the ways to go about in the task. The power of God is revealed where the multiplicity of gifts is recognised. Lawrence O. Richard says: "The Spirit is the quiet member of the Holy Trinity." Jesus said, "He will testify about me" (John 15:26). We do not pray to the Spirit, nor in the name of the Spirit, yet He is with us in our prayers—entering in, guiding, giving utterance and interpreting (Rom. 8:26-27). In the same way, the Spirit is with us in ministry. He gives gifts. He enables. He is the Minister in our ministry. In every basic way, you and I are simply expressions of God's Spirit. He is the One who reaches out through us to touch and heal. Building allegiance to the Spirit involves freeing each believer to live confidently as an expression of the Spirit. It means helping each believer trust the Spirit's presence enough to serve. [47]

The Spirit gives gifts, but is that all? As we try to understand and view the Spirit from the leadership development perspective, he does much more than that. In the process of bringing in an emerging and facilitating context, equipping and maturing by pruning, correcting and moulding, the Holy Spirit works through the leader also to equip others for the ministry. Thus, he brings obedience, trust, faith, wisdom and plans that are of and from God as well as enlarges both the ministry and ministry opportunities. The Holy Spirit's role thus remains crucial to the leadership development and maturing process. No leader ever will or can develop or function effectively apart from total dependence upon and submission and allegiance to the Holy Spirit. Otherwise, it is not spiritual leadership and not of God. The Holy Spirit in leadership or ministry development is, therefore, looking for men and women who will strive to develop spiritual leaders in the local church. They are leaders who are filled, led and guided by the Spirit, who would obey him as well as exercise the gifts endowed by him. "Spiritual leadership development is a key role of the Holy Spirit. He superintends, empowers, equips, directs, provides insights and delegates the authority to lead. It is His work."[48]

Conclusion

In this chapter, we discussed the biblical foundations of leadership training and development. We also discussed patterns of and means of leadership training and development. The chapter focussed on four major and distinct areas.

God develops a leader over a lifetime. The development is a function in the spheres of the outworking of events, people, time, circumstances and situations and leader responses and such to impress upon a leader in and by processing and integrating leadership lessons. Processing is central to the theory. All leaders can point to critical incidents in their lives where God taught them something very important.[49]

Leadership training of our Lord was focused on himself (John 14:9, 10) and on individuals (John 21). It was based on the Scriptures (Matt. 2:48f). It focused on an ultimate purpose and was based on the Father's will. These ingredients must be underscored, brought in and carefully integrated into the process of our pursuit of training, formation and developing matured servant-leaders for our day. The call, selection, training and equipping of leaders, importance of trainer or equipper and holistic development of leaders are all integral parts of this process.

The in-service, apprenticeship and on-the-job training over and against mere formal, cognitive, academic, theoretical and philosophical is to be given serious consideration. Or in other words, balancing these two components equally as two sides of one coin of the whole leadership development system and progress has much relevance.

We should have a renewed and enhanced approach to leadership situations, where we can combine both of these elements into the system. We must never forgo the earlier examples of the younger putting up with the older—mature, exemplary, godly and influential ones as apprentices, disciples and learners. Growing and emerging from there will be growing up for sure sustainable and lasting leadership. This calls for greater "life" and model than a mediocre and ordinary lifestyle.

Endnotes

[1] Clinton, *op. cit.*, p. 196.

[2] *Ibid.*, 40, 41.

[3] *Ibid.*, p. 245.

[4] *Lbid.*, p. 22.

[5] Raymur James Downey, *Old Testament Patterns of Leadership Training: Prophets, Priests and Kings.* Unpublished Th. M. Thesis submitted to Fuller Theological Seminary, 1981, p. 110.

[6] Clinton, *op. cit.*, p. 232.

[7] Sanders, *op. cit.*, p. 18.

[8] Sheldon H. Blank, *Understanding the Prophets,* New York: Union of Ameri-can Hebrew Congregation, 1969, p. 35ff.

[9] Johannes Lindblom, *Prophecy in Ancient Israel,* Philadelphia; Muhlenberg Press, 1962, p. 182.

[10] Watson David, *I Believe in the Church,* Grand Rapids: W. B. Eerdmans Co., 1978, p. 258.

[11] Raymur James Downey, *op. cit.,* p. 30

[12] Clinton, *op. cit.*, p. 15.

[13] Francis *Schaeffer, Joshua and the Flow of Biblical Ministry*, Downers Grove: Inter Varsity Press, 1975, p. 20.

[14] cf. Raymur Downey, *op. cit.*, p. 86.

[15] E. J. Young, *My Servants, The Prophets*, Grand Rapids: W. B. Eerdmans Co., 1952, p. 91.

[16] James Leon Wood, *The Prophet of Israel*, Grand Rapids: Baker Book House, 1979, p. 20.

[17] Francis Schaeffer, *op. cit.*, p. 25, 26.

[18] William Barclay, *The Mind of St. Paul*, New York: Harper & Row Publishers, 1959, p. 14.

[19] Raymur Downey, *op. cit.*, p. 96.

[20] "T. W. Manson, *The Teaching of Jesus: Studies of its Form and Context*, Cambridge: University Press, 1951, p. 240.

[21] Robert E. Coleman, *The Master Plan of Evangelism*, New Jersey: Fleming H. Revell Co., 1963, p. 21.

[22] C. Jinton, *op. cit.*, p. 106.

[23] Michael Youssef, *The Leadership Style of Jesus*, Wheaton: Victor Books.1986, p. 16.

[24] Coleman, *op. cit.*, p.33.

[25] John Kirkpatrick, *A Theology of Servant Leadership*, Unpublished D.Miss. Dissertation submitted to Fuller Theological Seminary, 1988, p. 275.

[26] Alexander Hay, *The New Testament Order for Church and Missionary*, Buenos Aires: N. T. Missionary Union, 1947, p. 41.

[27] Arthur Glasser, *Biblical Theology of Mission Syllabus*, Pasadena: Unpublished, 1988, p. 42.

[28] *Ibid.*

[29] Raymer Downey, *op. cit.*, p. 110.

[30] Coleman, *op. cit.*, p. 80.

[31] Alexander Balmain Bruce, *The Training of the Twelve*, New Canaan: Keats Publishing Inc., 1979, p. 30.

[32] Lawrence Richards, A *Theology of Christian Education*, Grand Rapids: Zondervan Publishing House, 1975, p. 159.

[33] Roland Allan, Missionary Methods: St. Paul's or Ours? Grand Rapids: W. B. Eerdmans Publishing Co., 1962, p. 95-102.

[34] Dean S. Gilliland, *Pauline Theology and Mission Practice*, Grand Rapids: Baker Book House, 1983, p. 216.

[35] Joseph A. Grassi, A *World to Win, The Missionary Methods of Paul the Apostle*, Maryknoll, N.Y.: Maryknoll Publications, 1965, p. 147.

[36] Dean S. Gilliland, *op. cit.*, pp. 218-222.

[37] Howard Snyder, *Liberating the Church*, Downers Grove: Intervarsity Press, 1983, p. 247.

[38] *Ibid.*

[39] Howard A. Snyder, *The Community of the King*, Downers Grove: Inter Varsity Press, 1977, p. 77.

[40] Peter Wagner, *Your Church Can Grow*, Ventura: Royal Books, 1984, p. 63.

[41] Kenneth O. Gangel, *Building Leadership for Church Education*, Chicago: Moody Press, 1980, p. 87.

[42] Edgar J. Elliston, *Home Grown Leaders.* Pasadena: Unpublished Draft, 1988; pp. 128, 129.

[43] Michael Youssef, *op. cit.*, p. 156.

[44] Eddie Gibbs, *I Believe in Church Growth*, London: Hodder and Stoughton, 19cS5, p. 25.

[45] Synder, Liberating the Church, *op. cit.*, p. 249.

[46] Ronald W. Leigh, *Effective Christian Ministry*, Wheaton: Tyndale House Publishers, 1984, p. 12.

[47] Lawrence O. Richards, A *Theology of Church Leadership*, Grand Rapids: Zondervan Publishing House, 1980, p. 254.

[48] Elliston, *op. cit.*, p. 123.

[49] Clinton, *op. cit.*, p. 25.

Chapter 3

Servant Songs: Reflections on Qualities and Characteristics of Servant-Hood

We briefly traced the biblical foundations of leadership training, formation and development in the last chapter. In this section, we will focus on the 'Servant Songs'—passages in the Old Testament book of Isaiah. This will help us unearth specific qualities, nature and characteristics of servant-hood leadership in the Church. We will take the Servant Songs as a source and revelation of God in the Old Testament and obtain insights into servant leadership and qualities. Our conviction and assumption are that the Servant Songs make direct reference to Jesus Christ as interpreted in the Gospels and the rest of the New Testament narratives. As Alfred Martin writes:

> This characterization of Christ as the Servant of Jehovah, first brought out in this evangelical prophet, is expanded in the Gospels, especially in Mark, which thus shows a close connection with Isaiah, and is recognized by the Church of the book of Acts.[1]

Jesus Christ is depicted as the supreme model of a Servant both in the Old and New Testaments. Each Christian who follows him, then, is exhorted to reflect the servant-hood lifestyle in ministries and leadership as the supreme means to the Kingdom Cause.

It is good for us also to mention here that there have been heated discussions, arguments and detailed studies on the Servant Songs and Deutero-Isaiah (chapters 40-55). Doubtlessly, reasonable and sincere questions may arise about these passages. Needless to say, so much study still needs to be done on these passages. Nevertheless, we will depend on a simple and plain approach to the material with the conviction that "all Scripture is inspired and is given for our instruction" in order to meet the objective and purpose of our study in this chapter.

Israel My Servant

The people of Israel were to be a special possession of God among all peoples. They were called to enter into a covenant with him marked with an unconditional obedience. The election of Israel was a channel by which the knowledge of God was to be brought into the world. They were to be a light to the nations. As Arthur Glasser says:

> Israel was appointed to be a "kingdom of priests" to enable the nations to enter the fullness of his salvation and blessing as the shalom of Yahweh. Actually, sinful Israel herself needed this shalom. It would remain for the suffering Servant to fulfil and consummate the sacrificial system when through the eternal Spirit He offered Himself without blemish to God...to put away sin by the sacrifice of Himself.[2]

Amos says: "You only have I known of all the families of the earth; therefore, I will punish you for all your iniquities" (Amos 3:2). Specially chosen by YHWH to be his servants and as instruments of blessing to all the nations, Israel forgot that this privilege also called for a great responsibility, commitment and obligation. The people of Israel often turned away from a theocentric rule and drifted away from the purpose of God for and through them to the nations. God has raised the prophets who will speak against injustice, exploitation of the poor, pride, sin, oppression and such uncharacteristic nature so that Israel would keep themselves within God's plan for the nations. Social injustice was a major theme of the message of the prophets. And sadly, the Lord had to punish them for their sins by sending them into exile.

It is from this background that the prophecies of Deutro-Isaiah have arose. "These chapters can be assigned with confidence to the period of Israel's exile in Babylon, for they presuppose its conditions, and promise a speedy deliverance from them."[3] George Knight puts it in the following way:

> It would surely be strange then if God had omitted to raise up a prophet at the vitally significant moment of the return from Exile, since this marks the climax of Israel's historical experience. Moreover, each one of the Old Testament prophets spoke out of the midst of a situation in which they were wholly involved, bodily, mentally, and spiritually, in the crisis in question. The prophets took no balcony view of events...as they all faced the particular situation together...their own minds were to work fruitfully upon the events which they knew God meant them to interpret.[4]

The central theme of the prophet in the passage is the "Servant of Yahweh", who will establish his cause for the nations by taking the role of a servant as was intended in the call of God for the people of Israel. These songs have great and direct implications in the New Testament for Jesus Christ, since Jesus is perceived as the supreme and perfectly obedient Servant. This lifestyle then needs to be initiated in the daily life of Christians who are called out to be witnesses of salvation of the Lord to the people of the world under the evangelical and cultural mandate.

Who Is the Servant?

The scholars suggest that the Hebrew word for servant means "slave," which originally meant that the inferior will naturally be the slave of the superior (Gen. 42:13: 2 Kings 8:13). This was also the nature of the people approaching God as found in Psalm 116:16. All of Israel were to be God's slaves and were to serve him (Exod. 3:12).

However, all are not called the Servant of God. The Israelites as a whole were called to serve God, yet only a few are distinguished and entitled 'My Servant,' which was great and an exceptional honour. Abraham (Gen. 26:12), Moses (Exod. 14:31), David (2 Sam. 7:5-8), Caleb (Num. 14:24), Elijah (2 Kings10:10) and the prophets (Amos 3:7) were a few of those distinguished ones of the Old Testament. "These were men who had a special task to perform and were all believed to know God's mind more deeply than other men did."[5]

The identity of the Servant is often questioned, for not every detail of these poems fits Jesus of Nazareth (e.g. inhuman appearance, grave with the wicked). To think that Isaiah foresaw Jesus of Nazareth is to misunderstand the nature of the Old Testament prophecy, according to some, for it had no immediate reference. Is it the people of Israel then? The songs suggest that this is Israel, though, within the songs themselves, it is somewhat obscure. At times, the prophet seems to be thinking of the faithful group in Israel, whereas on other occasions, he must be thinking of some individual even when the faithful group failed to listen and to obey.[6]

Who then would the Servant be? Some great figures in the Old Testament like Moses, David, Isaiah, Jeremiah and Jehoachim were men who were willing to offer their lives for the cause of the people and had characteristics in common with that of the Lord. It is used to refer to Isaiah himself (Isa. 20:3), Eliakim (Isa. 22:20), David (Isa. 37:35), Cyrus (Isa. 42:1-4), Jacob/

Israel (Isa. 42:23-25) and primarily to the 597 exiles or all of the Babylonian exiles. Jehoachim, for instance, was unjustly condemned and imprisoned. It is considered by many scholars that the individual spoken of by the prophet had not yet come when he wrote. However, this could involve three primary factors. Morna Dorothy Hooker says:

> First, the group can be spoken of as an individual; secondly, an individual member of the group can represent the whole society; thirdly, because the group includes the individual, and the individual represents the group, there is a fluidity in the concept which makes it possible to pass from an individual to the group of which he is a member and back again without any straining of the idea.[7]

Israel as a whole failed to respond to the call of God to be his servant, though a faithful group remained. Therefore, the task of bringing back a people who have strayed from God has to be the task of an obedient and dedicated individual. This person, when he appears, will be 'true' Israel or a representation of a new obedient Israel, the perfectly obedient Servant who in himself sums up the full meaning of "Israel my Servant." Maybe, the identity of the Servant is left unclear by Isaiah so as to emphasise the instrumentality of those who will be used by YHWH as "a light to the Nations." Glasser writes:

> Each intimation Jesus made of His death reflects some specific detail of the Servant of Yahweh as atoning sacrifice, portrayed in Isaiah 53. The cross is the culmination of salvation history: God's redemptive dealings with His people. His institution of the Eucharist, with its 'cup of the new Covenant,' reminds us of God's 'new Covenant' promised through Jeremiah (31:31 with Ezek. 36:24-28). His allusions to drinking wine with his people at the eschatological feast in the Kingdom of God likewise stamp him as the Suffering Servant (Mark 14:22-25; Luke 22:18).[8]

Songs of the Suffering Servant

Let us do a brief study of each of the Servant Songs. The four outstanding passages of the Servant Songs should be considered in order to plainly trace the picture of the Servant. These passages are Isaiah 42:1-4, 49:1-6, 50:4-9 and 52:13-53:12. In these songs, the mission of the Servant is significant and profoundly expressed.

In *the first song*, the Servant is identified as the instrument of God's purpose, endowed with Yahweh's Spirit; his task is to bring justice, righteousness and law upon the earth. The world mission of Israel to spread the cause of Yahweh is particularly stressed here. We must take note mainly of two concepts. Israel is the elect, the chosen one, for the simple reason that God has fallen in love with her. This underlines God's sole delights in Israel. The Servant's task is to publish *mispat*, which is rendered as law, the true law, the expression of Yahweh's will as the true religion. This is a function that exceeds any king or prophet. Christopher North states:

> Whether the Servant is to exercise the ministry of a travelling preacher, or to publish *mispat* after the fashion of a ruler issuing edicts, is not said. The concluding verse of the Song suggests the former, a task that will require unwearied patience; but taken by itself the phrase suggests decisions uttered by someone vested with executive authority. His authority may be exercised mildly—"A bruised reed he shall not break"—but the implication is that he could be severe if he wished.[9]

In the *second song*, the Servant himself is speaking, and the Servant is given a mission both to his own people and to the world. The Servant's call is explicit in this song, and the call is directed to bring the people of Israel out of exile. Therefore, it is the call to a specific individual who can be identified by name, and that name is Israel (cf.43:1). The Servant is mentioned as one whose mouth has been made like a sharp sword (49:2). The Servant must learn to be the instrument of the Word, and the Word should be carried out effectively to people in dungeons and darkness by a willing Servant. Three phrases found in verse 3 are of importance here: (1) "And he said to me", (2) "You are my Servant, Israel" and (3) "In whom I will be glorified." The function of the Servant is to reflect the light and glory of God as it strikes on a polished surface (John 17:1). The Servant is also depicted as a "light to the nations" who is to bring the salvation of the Lord to the ends of the earth (vs.67). Knight puts the concepts in the following way:

> What we have is the servant-group Israel seeking to re-establish and restore the whole Servant-people Israel to their rightful place in the plan and purpose of God. Then again when a congregation regains its understanding of the world mission of the church...its greater task is "to be my salvation to the ends of the earth."[10]

Whatever the identification or personification, hitherto our interest is to learn that the true Servant of Yahweh is to bring salvation to the people of the world. In this respect of the task, the Servant may face frustration and disappointment. He begins with his own people and then to the nations. "The primary calling in the first Song, then, and the ultimate calling in the second, is to the heathen. The ministry to Israel is subsidiary, and, as it were, by the way."[11] It is Jesus Christ of Nazareth as the Servant who brought salvation to the ends of the earth. The servant-people of God are his reflection today.

The *third song* records the Servant's response to the whole plan of Yahweh. The suffering and contempt of the Servant also appear vividly in this. A wholly dedicated Servant speaking is the image given in this passage. The Servant is aware of his need to learn and the humility to confess that need (vs.4). The Servant is pictured as one who is totally obedient and has learned not to rebel and run away or even to hit back. This is the hallmark of obedience and humility demonstrated by the Servant. It is Yahweh who teaches the Servant (v.5) and gives help in being so (v.7). In this song, we also "discover that the Servant's secret is an inner spring of joy and assurance."[12] In other words, this song ends "on a note of perfect trust in Yahweh, and of complete confidence in the ultimate issue."[13]

The *fourth song* is the longest of all. This presents us at least four features of the Servant. First of all, the individuality of the Servant is vivid. Secondly, the Servant, through his vicarious sufferings, has brought atonement to the sinners. Thirdly, the death is accepted voluntarily. It is an unjust death but is according to the divine will. And fourthly, somewhere and somehow the Servant is to be vindicated and is to survive death and be exalted. There is no doubt that the New Testament writers interpreted the Old Testament Servant passages as portraying Jesus Christ and we accept them based on authentication of the New Testament. It is very clear that the prophet Isaiah looked forward to some person who would give active expression to these qualities. We cannot say if he actually saw the Jesus who came. The description of the Gospel writers of the passion of our Lord Jesus Christ, the lifestyle of the servant-people of God and the ministries of the Church is the direct application in this regard. In the following statement, Alfred Martin stresses this point:

> This is not Isaiah who is speaking, nor is it an idealised portrait of the nation of Israel. It is an individual, not a group; it is The Servant; it is the Lord Jesus Christ (Matt.6:67; 27:30). These and a number of other passages show the applicability of the prophecy in Isaiah to the Lord Jesus Christ and to Him exclusively... It gives to us a wonderful prophetic picture of the sufferings and the death of the Lord Jesus Christ...this chapter reveals to us in greater measure than any other portion of the book the suffering of the Servant.[14]

The Song implies also that the Servant shall be effective and wise in winning many to righteousness and eternal life. This is to provide them with a wholly new view of life in accordance with the Torah (42:1). But it will be enunciated by one whose *"mien* is inhumanely marred." The song describes an actual death and burial of the Servant. And at the end, it foretells resurrection, portion with the great and prosperity.

Let us conclude our discussion with a few more reflections. The first song points to the Servant and hints that his task will not be easy. The second song pictures the Servant's commission, that is, to bring salvation to the ends of the earth by remaining the mouthpiece of Yahweh. In the third song, we see the Servant's endowment, learning humbly from Yahweh. Yahweh is his advocate and help while he goes through the suffering obediently and confidently. And finally, the fourth song pictures the suffering Servant, who in his vicarious suffering and unjust suffering, remains gentle and uncomplaining. In the end, he is given a portion with the great. This is the Servant! The servants of God have to partake in these sufferings, in the *diakonia*, and are to manifest ultimately this character of the Servant.

Jesus the Servant
The discussion so far has provided us with a good foundation and pointedness making strong implications to Jesus Christ and the New Testament ministry of the people of God. We should now briefly look into what Jesus conceived as his vocation in connection to these passages. According to Jesus, it is doubtless that the Servant mentioned in Isaiah was called to a great mission that consisted of three things: He must obey, he must witness and he must suffer. By doing so, he would be carrying out God's redemptive purpose for the world.

Jesus as the Servant
Jesus began his ministry by the announcement of the kingdom of God (Mark 1:14-15), which has a direct connection to the passages found in Isaiah, where "herald of good tidings" is connected closely to the word "gospel" (Isa. 40:9, 52:7, 61:1; Luke 4:17-18). By this, certainly, Jesus is claiming to be the messenger of God. Hanson writes:

> It is clear that Jesus identified himself with the 'herald of good tidings of Second Isaiah. In the time of exile the task of that herald was to announce the good news of the coming of the Kingdom of God, and in so doing identified himself with God's purpose as foreshadowed in Second Isaiah's prophecy.'[15]

The passage in Isaiah 42:6, where the prophet says, "I have given you as a covenant to the people, a light to the nations, to open the eyes that are blind", is directly symbolised as the "blood of the covenant" in instituting the Lord's Supper (Mark 14:24). A holy servant-leader is a mighty weapon in the hand of God who brings people to make covenant with God himself. This "...portrays the servant not as a general factotum, but as fulfilling specific tasks and embarking upon a special mission... It is God who sets him to these tasks and equips him for them."[16]

The Gospels have an array of depiction of Jesus as the Servant. Mark 10:43-45 is one of the great passages in this regard. In Luke 22:27 and 37, Jesus himself is identified as a servant, who would fulfil the redemptive work of God in the supreme example of service to God, which consists in giving his life for others as found in Isaiah 53. Though the Greek word rendered in Mark 10:43-45 for "servant" is not directly seen in Deutero-Isaiah, "...it is very difficult to imagine where Jesus derived the thought of service, if not from the Second Isaiah."[17] Colin Kruse says:

> Jesus was aware of the servant character of his ministry, and that he knew and used the servant-prophecies of Deutero-Isaiah... Mark 10:45 indicates what servant-hood meant to Jesus. It meant both lowly service rendered to mankind and a vicarious death on its behalf...substitutionary ideas are clearly present... There the servant bears two things on behalf on others: their sins and the punishment which resulted upon them.[18]

Thus, we see that both the ideas of servant-hood and vicarious suffering are brought together in the service of the Servant of the Lord. The service done to human beings—even to a little one, says Jesus—is done to him. Therefore, we can assume that service to Yahweh and to a very lowly person are similar and symbolically used. There are other references also that can be brought out from Deutero-Isaiah directly pertaining to the Gospels (Luke 22:27; Mark 9:12, 35; Isa. 53:3, 12).

Another interesting study in this section is that of there are corresponding passages in the Gospels where Jesus strongly encourages his disciples to be servants. The lessons along this line are very strong. The emphasis on humility, supremely shown in the Master and to be reflected in the disciples, is absolutely central in Jesus' conception of his own vocation; the disciples are called to be the extensions of the same in the world. There are many references to the suffering of Jesus in the Gospels directly quoted from the Old Testament; to suffer and die is necessary and helps carry out God's purpose for his people (Mark 8:27-37, 9:30-31, 10:32-34). The other Gospel narratives also have said in this regard (Luke 12:50, 13:32-34; Matt. 23). The terrible denunciation of the scribes and the Pharisees found in Matthew 23, a dark chapter in the Gospels, ends by summing up Israel's history as full of disobedience and rebellion. Saint Matthew clearly implies that their alienation from God reaches its climax in the death (killing) of the Messiah himself. Matthew 23:35 says that "... upon you may come all the righteous bloodshed on earth, from the blood of innocent Abel to the blood of Zachariah, the son of Barachiah, whom you murdered between the sanctuary and the altar."

Israel as the servant of God was called to listen and obey God speaking through his prophets. The prophet then went on to think of a faithful group who would carry out the task of the Servant by his voluntary suffering and death. Hanson says it well:

> The significance of 'all the righteous bloodshed upon earth' is summed up and expressed in the death of the Servant in just the way that the rejection and suffering of all the prophets is summed up and brought to fruition in the suffering and death

of Jesus. The prophets were God's servant if anyone was, and in the death of Jesus the meaning of the deaths of both the Servant and the Servants is finally understood.[19]

Further, we can draw principles very common to the characteristics of Servant leadership from the above verses. These verses do not emphasise the status or the function of the disciples, but emphasise the Servant's attitude that should be centre to their relationships with each other. A servant-leader cannot expect anything better than what the Master has gone through. The servants are expected to be faithful to their masters. In the execution of the tasks, another essential principle is stressed. What Jesus has said to the disciples is relevant in this regard; he says that "a disciple is not above his teacher, nor a servant above his master; it is enough for the disciple to be like his teacher, and the servant like his master" (Matt. 10:24). This shows another picture of the Jesus' style of leadership, that is, the significance is not in the "promotion of the disciples to the rank of their teacher, but the readiness to bear the same abuse which the teacher and master encountered and to accept it as a rank of supreme distinction."[20]

The servant is not a passive sufferer but an active subject as God's instrument, in God's plan. This is servant leadership! The scholars refer to the title "Servants of God" as a "term of honour for the prophets and possibly even to the Servant of God," the Messiah who, in fact, set a higher example of the leader in contrast to all existing norms of the master-servant relationship.

Both the church of Jesus Christ and the Head of the church, Jesus Christ himself, are today looking for those who will take "the form of a servant" in "serving" the people and "being" will make the core of their ministry. Leaders are, therefore, men and women who are prepared for lowly and humble service to one another. And if the servant-character of Jesus' ministry is the pattern for us today, which is in fact inevitable, is it incorrect to say that the prophecies of Deutero-Isaiah are to find fulfilment in our leadership and ministries as well? These servant qualities are absolute and ought to be reflected in the ministries of his servants, too. "This would mean that Jesus viewed the disciples not only as his servant but also as fellow-servants of God together with him."[21] Servant leadership is the living out of the life of Jesus by us as co-labourers with God the Father through the grace and power that abounds from His Holy Spirit.

Vocation of Jesus
The scholarly attempts to identify Jesus with the Servant of the prophet Isaiah have raised many questions about whether Jesus himself saw him as the Servant. Whether one approves or disapproves, it is beyond doubt that life and ministry of Jesus remarkably fits into the passages in Isaiah. Three duties of a servant as stated earlier, namely, obedience, witness and suffering, are all prominent themes in the life of Jesus as well.

His duty of obedience is clearly viewed by the Father at the time of baptism and is followed by his obedience in temptation and through his earthly ministry. The baptism of Jesus demonstrates deep and strong allegiance and the confession of his deep commitment to the commission of the Father in service. This reveals his willingness to suffer as a servant. What began at first with the astounding historical narrative of his incarnation is now confirmed by his voluntary choice. In this way, suffering is an instrumentality in God's purpose, or in other words, servant-hood includes suffering. We are not designed to serve a theory, even a true theory. Theories enslave. The truth is that our model is Jesus, the person who became human, possibly to the extent that he could not have been more human. He was humble and lowly, but was yet a wonder by his obedience, total allegiance, loyalty and commitment to the calling. This is the vocation of a servant-leader and the lifestyle that must undergird his or her actions and purposes.

Jesus' ministry of witness is also seen clearly in the Gospels. "For this I was born, and for this I have come into this world, to bear witness to the truth" (John 18:37). As Jesus began to proclaim the good news of the Kingdom, he started out with the verses we read in Isaiah 61:1-2; and adds: "Today this Scripture has been fulfilled in your hearing" (Luke 4:18-21). Thus the message of Jesus was interlinked with his vocation as was the subject of suffering. He was witnessing the good news of the Kingdom to the poor, broken-hearted, down-trodden, dejected, rejected, hated and hopeless and to the pharisaic group and society. The vocation or witness was thus to identify with the people and to raise them up to be hopeful. Hanson writes:

> Jesus saw himself as the heir of Israel's destiny. God sends to them a succession of Servants; these must represent the prophets and the righteous men whose blood has been shed in the past by disobedient Israel. Finally, he sends his Son and him the tenants put to death. Because of this, the vineyard will be given to others. Once again, the destiny of the servants has culminated in the destiny of Jesus. The new Israel that is to be born in him.[22]

John 13 explicitly states that the Holy Eucharist and washing the disciple's feet go together or one precedes the other. An attitude of humble service, seen as the focus in life, was also to be the keynote in the lives of the disciples. The thirteenth chapter of John declares the style of leadership on which our own life is to be founded. The vocation of Jesus was accomplished in a humble attitude that must have been opposite to the normal pattern that his disciples understood from their times and world. Greenslade writes:

> Any leader who follows his master in this will be radical and prophetic in his thrust and will inevitably disrupt the polite

diplomacy and cautious consensus that passes for wisdom in most church circles. Above all, a realisation of sonship brings an immense sense of security that Jesus felt so free to serve as the lowest slave in washing the feet of his disciples.[23]

Reading through the beginning of the chapter will help us to realise that Jesus was fully aware of his identity of being the Son of God in position, authority and ministry; and was uninhibited by self-consciousness when he bowed down to wash the feet of his followers. He is our example of leadership. We should be far from striving for our position in order to fulfil our calling. We need to risk the misunderstanding of others and should be prophetic in what we do. "We will be freed to act prophetically at the risk of being misunderstood. We will have no need to waste emotional energy on vindicating ourselves."[24] For we do not preach ourselves, but Jesus Christ as Lord, and ourselves as your servants for Jesus' sake (2 Cor. 4:5). Jesus deliberately chose the lowest position of servant-hood. He expects the same role from all of his leaders at all times and everywhere.

After this demonstration of servant-hood, Jesus asked his disciples, "Do you know what I have done to you?" (v.12). And he said to them, "You call me teacher and Lord, and you are right, for so I am. If then, your Lord and teacher has washed your feet, you also ought to wash one another's feet. For I have given you an example, that you also should do as I have done to you" (vs. 13-15). Jesus was training those who were to be future leaders taking his place after he was gone. And this remained a strong lesson on leadership. The popular world may describe it to be a tragedy. But Jesus Christ desires that such should be the leaders of His church—those who will follow his example. The "servant-hood" does not obliterate the divine authority of the one who is sent to serve, for "he who receives you, receives me," said Jesus. None of us must assume that our authority in anyway is lessened or put to nought when our leaders become servant-like. Bishop K. P. Yohannan writes to this effect:

> Christian leadership and service are not hierarchical, even though many of our current organizations are organized along worldly lines of power. The Kingdom is not patterned after corporate America or military. Instead, it is a fellowship of servants in which we are to let the servant-mindset of Christ become our mind.[25]

Also, it seems that the word *Eucharistia* used for "thanksgiving" by Paul in 2 Corinthians 4:15 should tell us that John, in including here the service with the institution of the Lord's Supper, means that there is a strong notion that the Church's sacramental worship is altogether a service. This, in fact, should follow humble service abounding with thanksgiving even in our sufferings and pain to the extent that the mystery of Christ is communicated through them to the world.

We can, therefore, conclude that Saint John understood the Servant Songs as a description of Christ himself. A comparative look into the concept of "lifting up" and "glorifying" from the passages of Servant Songs in Isaiah and the gospel of John explicitly points to the identity of Christ as the Servant of the Lord (Isa. 49:3, 52:13; compared with John 3:15, 12:32-34, 13:31-32, etc.). Concerning this passage, Glasser says:

> By this act of lowly service, he dramatized his role as the unique Servant of God and called His disciples to put servant-hood at the heart of their understanding of the ministry. In so doing, he underscored the role of the servant as pre-eminent within the Kingdom of God... This means that He not only gladly served people, but embraced and carried out the awesome tasks of reconciling them to God through his life of obedience and his submission to death.[26]

Thus Jesus' ministry provides us with a unique pattern of service, motivation and impulse—that of serving others. Jesus, therefore, carries out in his person and life the obedient service

God has required of the people of Israel. In and through the history of Israel, the destiny of God's faithful and the destiny of the servants of the Lord are supremely expressed in the destiny of the 'One Servant' who gave his life as a ransom for many. Active service, prophetic ministry, a future-orientation and hope towards a coming Kingdom and the authority in Jesus Christ have been a certain design in God's plan for all nations.

Witness of the New Testament

Gleaning through the epistles, we gain valuable insights into what it meant for the early church to declare and believe that Jesus is the Servant-Messiah.

The passages selected for this study are Philippians 2, Romans 10 and 15 and 1 Peter. The Philippians passage certainly has a close link to Isaiah 53. A thorough and in-depth understanding of the phrases, "emptied himself'" and "poured out his soul unto death" brings a great toll to this learning.

Paul refers to Christ as the Servant in Romans 15:7-12. This passage says that God had always desired that Israel would receive their Messiah and that the Gentiles also would come through the Messiah to worship God. The way to achieve this purpose was accomplished by the Messiah becoming a Servant. Three lessons stand out in both of these passages: Christians are encouraged to mutual love, incarnational life is central to everything and humiliation and suffering of Christ are prominent. Christ is pictured as speaking in the words of the Old Testament (c.f. Isa. 45:23). And in both, the glory of the Father is the ultimate end. Therefore, Hanson says, "Christ's being a servant was an essential part of his redemptive action in St. Paul's view, and this view was not peculiar, it was part of the tradition of the church as he knew it."[27]

The letter of 1 Peter also presents an awesome picture of the theme, "Servant of the Lord." Jesus Christ the Servant is the theme running throughout the book. Obedience, humility, sympathy, love, a tender heart, a humble mind, patience, an absence of revenge, a clear conscience and unjust sufferings are depicted as an ideal of Christian conduct and projected and deeply embedded in the life of Jesus Christ. This is very clear as Peter states, "Live as free men, yet without using your freedom as a pretext for evil; but live as servants of God... For to this you have been called because Christ also suffered for you, leaving you an example that you should follow in his steps" (1 Pet. 2:16, 21).

Qualities of the Servant

The first and foremost quality is the call of God, which may also be framed as selection or God's approval (Isa. 42:1, 49:2, 3, 5). Examples of this are countless both in the Bible and the history of Christian missions. This may be a pre-natal call on the Servant's life. In his book, Michael Youssef, underscores it as the first principle of the leadership style of Jesus. He says, "Jesus received confirmation before he could lead. So must we."[28] This needs to be underscored—while we can provide thoroughfare training for leadership and development, only God calls. Currently, we find that there are many who are skilled and talented, professionals, good performers and informed people serving in many positions and capacities in the kingdom's work. Sadly, we want instant performers, computer literates and those who are competent in "performing." But their life and ministries may lack spiritual vitality and fervour, and organisation and institutions whom they lead may not have the godliness and divine protection since they are not called and assigned by God.

Second, the Servant is cleansed and sanctified by God. This is synonymous with consecration and purity in the Bible. "I was not rebellious" (Isa. 50:5) directly conveys that the Servant is purified for a higher purpose by cleansing, which brings an obedient heart. Only God can cleanse his Servant (Ps. 51:10;

Job.14:4). As they were initiated by God to be an instrument and His word to the people, so were they cleansed by God. He will never use a defiled vessel for a holy purpose (Isa. 49:2).

Third, the Servant is commissioned by God (Isa. 42: 1, 2). The call infers and reveals the commission as well (49:1 b). Isaiah 49:3, 6 says, "You are my Servant. ...I will give you as a light to the nations" and later, "Behold my Servant. ..." (52:13). Commissioning also shows that the Servant is set apart for a peculiar purpose and task and that the Servant is committed to do only God's will. This commissioning, however, results in an immense reservoir of authority and power for the task itself.

Fourth, the Servant is preserved by God (Isa. 42:4). "He will not fail or be discouraged until he had established justice on the earth" sufficiently indicates that the Servant is preserved by God. Otherwise, the exhausting tasks of the Servant could have been discouraging and heavy and may not be accomplished. Being preserved from such causes determines the protection of God. This concept also signifies the idea that the Lord is the Servant's strength (49:5c). The assurance of the Servant being guarded from shame, defeat and guilt indicates that the preservation is of divine origin. It is said, therefore, "for the Lord God helps me... I know I shall not be put to shame; he who vindicates me is near" (50:7). There are startling examples that we can draw from the Bible regarding this point. Because of this soul-lifting assurance, the Servant is able to say, "Yet surely my right is with the Lord, and my recompense with my God" (49:4b). This strong sense of preservation from God can help us in servant-leadership to hold onto two principles that Youssef states: "In Christ's Service I can have courage for every leadership battle... Leaders who are secure in Jesus Christ have nothing to protect."[29]

Fifth, the servant is empowered by God. See the phrases such as "I have put my spirit upon him" (42:1). "He made my mouth like a sharp sword...my God has become my strength" (49:2, 5c), "so shall he startle many nations; kings shall shut their mouths because of him" (52:15). The patient and obedient manner in which he bore all struggles as seen in chapter 53 are strong indicators that the power of God has been upon the Servant. No servant can do anything for God's kingdom with their natural power, endowments and charisma, without divine empowerment. As the servant in Deutero-Isaiah, many of God's servants have to face hostile situations, oppositions and demonic forces in their service; and it would be impossible to "see through" apart from the power on high. This is the touch of the supernatural, the anointing of the Holy Spirit created to stir up the effectiveness of a servant-ministry. This is indispensable!

Sixth, the Servant is guided by God, which means led by God. This is one of the major emphases throughout the Bible. The people of Israel were led by God, by clouds during the day and by the pillar of fire at night. Their leaders, such as Moses and Joshua, were guided by God in all circumstances, along with the prophets and the apostles. Servants of the Lord 'waited' for God's sovereign leading and guidance. The leading of the Lord comes supernaturally and through other means. He leads them through his servants, his word, special inspiration, visions and revelations. The servant-leader is successful only as he or she heeds the guiding of the Lord. Unquestionably, one true servant-leader with God's guidance and help is greater than a strong majority.

Seventh, the Servant is humble in service. This concept is repeatedly seen in the Servant Songs. It should be of central importance to all servant-leadership. A few references to these aspects are cited: 42:2, 3; 50:4, 5, 53:7, 8. Humility also could be studied in terms of lowliness, meekness and submission. Some equate meekness with weakness and consider it as negative a quality. But the Bible does not teach so. In fact, it is quite the opposite. The Bible tells us that humility goes before exaltation (1 Pet. 5:5). "Meekness is a quality of strength and spiritual authority which causes the leader to be under control and subject to the will of God at all times."[30] The servant-leader would never misinterpret the esteemed quality of humility. We need to soak ourselves in and maintain an attitude of humility of Jesus our Lord. Humility is the hallmark of service to God. So, the higher the leadership position, the greater the humility.

Eighth, another typical characteristic of a servant of God is the rejection and scorn faced by the world (50:6; 53:3). This is not necessarily a "must" quality of the servant-leader. But rejection, dejection, hurt, despise, being misunderstood, opposition, unfairness, loneliness and lack of appreciation are normal and part of the life and ministry of a servant, because this is the way the world manifests itself to the servant—Jesus Himself. Isaiah was rejected and harassed by his own countrymen (8:11). Jeremiah underwent unbearable oppression from his own people (1:19) and so did Daniel and many others. Suffering and rejection are normal and commonly expected elements in the ministry of a true servant-leader. But the servant continues with optimism and courage because in Christ's service the leader has courage for every leadership challenges.[31] Only a leader who has made a radical commitment and has selfless ambition can take such situations optimistically and live through them victoriously.

Ninth, the quality and attribute is that of gentleness and patience (53:7). "The Christian leader must not be pugnacious, but genial and gentle; not a contentious controversialist, but one who is sweetly reasonable."[32] A servant-leader should manifest a gentle approach and manner in all the dealings within the ministry and life. He should not have a wobbly and irrepressible temperament. A Christian leader should liberally be clothed with patience and be temperate for a sound leadership and in all undertakings and transactions. It is the far more competent virtue of forbearance and a Christ-like lifestyle that need to be embraced. A servant-leader requires patience in the realm of personal relationships because it is there that the most stringent test appears. This is also the ability of self-control (2 Pet. 1: 6). William Barclay puts it in the following way:

> The word never means the spirit which sits with folded hands and simply bears things. It is victorious endurance, masculine constancy under trial. It is Christian steadfastness, the brave and courageous acceptance of everything life can do to us, and the transmitting of even the worst into another step on the upward way. It is courageous and triumphant ability to bear things, which enables a person to pass breaking point and not to break, and always to greet the unseen with a cheer.[33]

So much of God's work is left undone and people have suffered because of hasty moves, decisions and lack of an enduring approach of leaders! A leader with impatient dispositions endangers and is a great enemy to growth and success and life of people. Sanders writes:

> The man who is impatient with weakness will be defective in his leadership. The evidence of our strength lies not in racing ahead, but in a willingness to adapt our stride to the slower pace of our weaker brethren while not forfeiting our lead.[34]

Many leaders tend to pass hasty judgements upon individuals who are very precious to God and by doing so hurt both the individuals and the work of God in those individuals. Such leaders forget that everything is in the hand of God and that their call is to lead all those whom God has put among and with them. After all, God is in the business of making individuals, not programmes and strategies. Let us acclaim that patience is one of the characteristics of the Servant and should be lived out in every practical aspect of the life of a servant-leader and in leadership functions.

Tenth, the Servant is without attraction and is probably opposite to the expectations and ways of appeal of a life in the world (52:14; 53:2). The servant-leader may exemplify that which is opposite or negative to the common ways of thinking and lifestyle. The world cries for attraction, which could be deceptive, whereas the Lord looks for eternally laid-down principles that may be contrary to the usual flow. This concept also goes so much in line with what we read in the first chapter of the epistle of 1 Corinthians.

Eleventh, the Servant is characterised as a light to the nations (49:6). This shows that the servant needs to bring salvation to the people. The Bible does not know or does not want to know a leader who has no heart and passion for those who do not know Jesus and His love for them. A true servant-leader is one whose every movement contributes something towards world renewal. This was the purpose of the Servant, Jesus Christ, who said that his purpose in life was to "give a ransom for many." This is a radical commitment, the way of the cross and forsaking all for the sake of Jesus and His kingdom.

Twelfth, the Servant is triumphant in mission (52:13, 53:10-12). The ultimate victory is the share of the Servant: "I will divide him a portion with the great", "he shall divide the spoil with the strong", "the will of the Lord shall prosper in his hand", "Behold, my Servant shall prosper, he shall be exalted and lifted up, and shall be very high" (53:10-12, 52:13). All of these phrases point towards the ultimate victory of the Servant. At the end, a servant shall be victorious, although the Servant is disfigured, portrayed contrary to popular thinking and normal flow of happenings. The total direction of the Servant's mission is based on this ultimate hope.

Practical Applications and Insights

First, the call of God is central to the mission of the servant. In any case, whether forced or led willingly into the service, the call of God is the basis for leadership; or to put it this way for a 'sustainable and godly leadership.' Much of the leadership struggles today seems to be because of those who are in leadership positions and ministry—because of their status, personal considerations and power—and not necessarily because of spiritual life and quality and the sense of personal call and conviction. They find all carnal means to achievement and success and represent ministry with wrong, ungodly motivations and principles. A constant cleansing of God and consecrating ourselves afresh to His service must be our attitude.

Second, dimension is the principle of obedience to what God instructs and learning just what God says. It is vital for extending leadership benefits to those whom we lead. The habit of complete obedience and submission to what God says is an essential virtue that leads to consistent progress in leadership and development. We strive hard at times to impress people with what we do; conversely, it often reflects wrong motives and attitudes. We strive for status, position and title; whereas the ministry is not an office, but a function.

The question to ponder is: Can we manifest the true Christian nature by our mutual and loving relationships with one another while striving for "status" and claim to be "zealous"? We must learn to be bond-slaves and have an attitude of service in every ministry situation; we must count it as an honour in itself. It is written that no one from the east or the west or from the desert can exalt a man. But it is God who judges; He brings one down, he exalts another (Ps. 75:6, 7).

Our authority or commission comes from God and it is based on our submission and obedience to him. He does empower us. The power struggles to climb up and sustain positions and titles are, therefore, pointless and unbiblical. It is by being a servant that the leader is called to exercise the authority entrusted by the Holy Spirit. For a leader whom God raises, promotion comes not from the west or the east or from the south. A leader should choose the very end of line and serve and still count it an honour. A servant means to serve; and this is called for even when one's position, power, titles and such are shaken or taken away. Such leaders remain faithful to God and the ministry and still serve without holding any partiality, personal interests and spirit of embitter and bias.

Servant-hood lifestyle never cancels the divine authority of the one who is sent to serve. For Jesus said, "He who receives you receives me." We must never look down upon a leader, if the leader or the emerging leader looks "innocent", "unskilled" or "servant-like." If one conducts and treats a leader so, it directly points to one's inner directives and attitude towards leadership and God the Master.

Our guide is God himself. He leads and guides us in truth into various spheres of ministry, providing new opportunities for witnessing, into new and great passion, goals and strategies. How genuine and consistent is our trust in our "Leader," the "Captain of our Salvation"? He fights the battle for us. His only expectation of us is to follow him patiently, faithfully and wholly along the path.

Gentleness and patience are the basic requirements of leaders in all their conduct and dealings. How gentle a shepherd are we to our sheep? How patient a leader are we to our followers? How quick and premature are we to pass on judgements upon those whom we suppose to lead? Is it not true to say that we have miserably failed God in these areas and have often brought shame to His glory and have even delayed His programmes by being a "dead fly in the ointment?"

Jesus was "all out" for service. He served on behalf of people and as a servant took this lowly state in identifying himself with the people. The emphasis is on humility and a contrite spirit. The servants of Jesus Christ are called to display humility in all aspects of their ministry as well. In order to be humble, one needs to have an open heart and a spirit of acceptance, equity and the 'other-mindedness' towards all. A leader should be committed to go beyond the personal horizon of judgements and rationalistic approach of viewing people and things. It might take one through sufferings, pain and hardships that are unsought for and are hard at times.

As shepherds of God's people, leaders should regularly ask the following soul-searching questions to find out where they stand: How much of a servant-heart do I possess as a leader? Do I embrace service and servant-hood as an indignity to the position of leadership? Are things like the dignity of my brother and sister—commonly speaking, the co-workers—and their call, ministry, vocations and status more important to me than personal agenda and zeal? Are progress, activities and projects, one's life of effectiveness, quality of life—the consistent, stable, firm and progressive lifestyle—my interest? Evaluation and success are not measured by human social values and standards. It is ultimately God who vindicates and measures success. A leader needs to be strong and trustworthy in following the Lord. Here lies the importance of the virtue of the contrite spirit that the Bible says God's people must possess. A whole-hearted and strong integration of a theology of suffering in leadership is basic to all these. Being a servant of God is not an easy task. The servant strives to serve the purpose of God, no matter what the cost is. This is the key to an effective and sustainable leadership.

Endnotes

[1] Alfred Martin, Isaiah - *The Salvation of Jehovah*, Chicago: Moody Press, 1956, p.71.

[2] Arthur Glasser, *op. cit.*, p. 77.

[3] Robinson Wheeler, *The Cross in the Old Testament*, Philadelphia: The Westminster Press, 1995, p. 67.

[4] George Knight, *Isaiah 40-45, Servant Theology*, Grand Rapids: W.B. Eerdmans Co., 1984, pp. 1-2.

[5] Anthony T. Hanson, *The Church of the Servant*, London: S.C.M. Press Ltd., 1962, p. 13.

[6] Christopher Richard North, *The Suffering Servant in Duetero-Isaiah*, London: Oxford University Press, 1948, p. 40-52.

[7] Morna Dorothy Hooker, *Jesus and the Servant*, London: SPCK, 1959, p. 42.

[8] Glasser, *op. cit.*, p. 17.

[9] North, *op. cit.*, pp. 141-142.

[10] George Knight, *op. cit.*, p. 31.

[11] North, *op. cit.*, p. 144.

[12] Knight, *op. cit.*, p. 146.

[13] North, *op. cit.*, p. 147.

[14] Alferd Martin, *op. cit.*, pp. 86, 89.

[15] Anthony Hanson, *op. cit.*, p. 30.

[16] Philip Greenslade, Leadership, *Greatness and Servanthood*, Minneapolis: Bethany House Publishers, 1984, p. 104.

[17] Anthony Hanson, *op. cit.*, p.31.

[18] Colon Kruse, *New Testament Models for Ministry: Jesus and Paul*, Nashville: Thomas Nelson Publishers, 1983, p. 45.

[19] Anthony Hanson, *op. cit.*, p. 36.

[20] Gunther Bornkamm, *Paul* (translated by D. M. G. Stolker), New York: Harper & Row Publishers, 1971, pp.144-45.

[21] Colin Kruse, *op. cit.*, p. 5l.

[22] Anthony Hanson, *op. cit.*, p. 38

[23] Philip Greenslade, *op. cit.*, pp.103, 104.

[24] Colin Kruse, *op. cit.*, p. 5l.

[25] K. P. Yohannan, *The Road to Reality,* Altamonte Springs: Creation House, 1988, p. 170.

[26] Glasser, *op. cit.,* p. 38.

[27] Anthony Hanson, *op. cit.,* p. 41.

[28] Michael Youssef, *op. cit.,* p. 17.

[29] *Ibid.,* pp. 48, 107.

[30] John William Kirkpatrick, *op.cit.,* p. 223.

[31] Michael Youssef, *op. cit.,* p. 48.

[32] Sanders, *op. cit.,* p. 54.

[33] William Barclay, *op. cit.,* p. 258.

[34] Sanders, *op. cit.,* p. 99.

Chapter 4
Pauline Insights into Leadership: Imitate Me

Many scriptural passages of Paul provide both explicit and implicit applications to leadership of our day. The letters to Timothy and Titus are worthy of a distinct treatment in this regard and are a good resource to rely upon. In this chapter, we will look at the following topics:

- Unique roles and partnership of Paul in leadership style
- Developing perspectives and a philosophy of the servant's identity and ministry from the selected Corinthian passages
- The call and commission of leaders to be ministers of reconciliation

This study is based upon the writings of the apostle Paul and the Lucan narrative of the Acts of the Apostles.

Paul was born in Tarsus in the region of Cilicia of the tribe of Benjamin. Not much is known about his family, apart from the fact that they must have been wealthy people, for he was born as a Roman citizen (Acts 16:37). It was probably at the age of thirteen that he came to Jerusalem to obtain training under Gamaliel, and he would have resided with his sister and family. He became extremely zealous for Jewish traditions and excelled in Jewish theology (Gal.1:14).

The Apostle Paul first appears in the book of Acts as a persecutor of the Church. He witnessed the martyrdom of Stephen, and he himself imprisoned Christians at Jerusalem, seizing men and women from their houses and committing them to prison (Acts 7, 8:1-3). What may have been his motivation in persecuting the Christians, we do not know. We do know that he obtained official letters from the high priest of Jerusalem to further persecute them and travelled to Damascus to seek out Jewish Christians (Acts 9:1-3). However, he experienced a radical change as he came to realise that he was opposing God in ignorance and unbelief and that zeal for God is not best presented in such expressions of service to him (1 Timothy 1:13). Later, he testified to the elders at Ephesus: "But I do not account my life of any value nor as precious to myself, if only I may accomplish my course and the ministry which I received from the Lord Jesus to testify to the gospel of the grace of God" (Acts 20:24).

Paul had a dramatic experience that turned around his life and its destiny. He was confronted by the risen and exalted Christ on the way to Damascus. A flashing light from heaven surrounded him and he was struck with blindness. He received a very personal revelation of Jesus Christ. The answer of Paul to the voice from heaven, "Saul, Saul, why do you persecute me?" was very direct. He asked in response, "Who are you, Lord?" The voice replied, "I am Jesus, whom you are persecuting" (Acts 9:3-6). For Paul, the conversion experience carried a memorable lesson—that God takes the initiative and humans in turn respond. This, then, became the beginning of an unparallel journey of this great personality of the New Testament times.

Leadership Roles of the Apostle Paul

Competent Teacher

Ephesians 4:11 describes pastor and teacher as one of the leadership gifts for the Church. Teaching was the heart of the Church-planting ministry for the Apostle Paul. He also instructed Timothy to entrust to the faithful people the things he had learned and seen (2 Timothy 2: 2). The apostle saw this as one of his great concerns, an essential ministry in the Church, and a quality prerequisite to be seen among church leaders (1 Titus 3:2, 4:13; 2 Timothy 2.2). An absence of constructive and wholesome teaching with a pursuit to build up is a major cause for immature, shallow and superficial Christianity of our today. One is to teach Christ the Truth. In order to teach the truth, one must combat error and untruth. Teaching for maturity will relate doctrine to life.[1]

The goal of Christian teaching is to bring all members of the Body into a ministering relationship with one another. "It is not simply the teaching of the Word that is important in Christian education. It is how the Word is taught."[2] Christian teaching is unique and that it is teaching for transformation— teaching designed to support the process of Christ-likeness in a believer. This is not simply training believers in what the leaders *know*, but helping them become what *leaders* are (Luke 6:40). The goal is to bring people to Christ-likeness by presenting a model or pattern in every aspect of the life of a teacher. This is where the competency of a leader-teacher is put to test and biblically measured.

The task is to present every believer mature in Christ (Col. 1:28). And it is a corporate task. The teacher himself first has to realise this truth before one can mobilise each believer towards this goal. The advice of Paul to the Colossians becomes significant in this regard, as he says, "teach and admonish one another" (Col. 3:16). Richards writes:

> ...leaders are the key to building the body into a functioning, ministering community. But first we must realize, and commit ourselves to the understanding of the local Body as a ministering fellowship. We must give fullest commitment to the Bible's teaching that there are NO "layman", that each of us is believer-priest.[3]

Believing Community is not empowered just with a pastoral office, but with a pastoral function. This is a shepherding function directed towards edification and the growth of the Church. Shepherding includes teaching. In both the educational and leadership principles, the teacher or leader is a model. In education, the learner is a disciple groomed to be like his or her teacher; so also in Christian leadership the believer is a priest becoming like the leader. In education and leadership, modelling and identification are the principal methods by which transformation takes place. Especially in leadership, modelling and identification are the examples by which leaders lead. In the educational principle, there is an "among" rather than "over" relationship between the leader and the led, which is transactional.[4]

Encouraging Spiritual Father

"Our experience of fatherhood can make or break our leadership."[5] Paul was a father to Timothy who seemingly needed constant exhortation and strengthening in faith. Paul calls Timothy his "true child in faith" (1 Tim. 1:2), which indicates that he related to him as a parent. He calls him, "beloved son" (2 Tim. 1:2). It was an expression of the fatherly affection of Paul for Timothy when he says, "I have no one like him, who is genuinely anxious for your welfare...how as a son (Php. 2:20, 21). Paul and Timothy walked, worked, lived and served together. Timothy was fortunate to observe firsthand the way Paul did things.

This was a fatherly model with examples and values of right motivation, upright living, high morale and ethic, great faith and the example of obedience and endurance. Paul, with great spiritual authority, could, therefore, advise Timothy, who was preparing for future leadership. Greenslade writes:

> In every respect this father-son relationship which Paul and Timothy enjoyed is a model of how brother should love one another and of how an experienced leader can develop and train a potential leader. When men of God "father" others in the ways of God we are on the safe road to the next generation of leadership. By this method, if it can be called that, we will transmit life and vision not merely theories and ideas. The church desperately needs more fathers with this stature.[6]

The apostle demonstrates a relational style of leadership in this through his bonded relationship with him. Paul cultivated and maintained such a strong relationship with all those whom he led to the Lord (1 Th. 2:11, 12; 1 Cor. 4:14-16; Phm. 10-12). It is not necessarily a 'dependent relationship,' but an ongoing concern for the maturity, progress and well-being of the followers. It is taking on other people's problems in a patriarchal concern and prayer.

Self-sacrificing Mother

This picture of a leadership role goes in line with the concept already mentioned. However, in this is revealed a greater affection, care and sacrifice that a natural mother would give her child. Paul likens himself to a "mother" (1 Th. 2:7, 8; Gal. 4: 1 9; 1 Col. 3: 1, 2). He says that like a mother who travails to give birth to a child, his longing and desire for seeing people transformed and accept faith in Jesus Christ was so great and deep. This is not only bringing people to birth, but also mothering and nursing them to growth and maturity. This role embodies and ensures a lifestyle and quality of tenderness and sensitivity in a relationship characterised in a true mother to bring growth and be reproductive. Leaders with this quality will make all efforts to see their followers comforted on every side, not their own comforts, positions and achievements, but those of the followers. It is here that a real sacrificing quality is required (Isa. 66:13) Every leadership action, decision, moves and steps, planning and strategies, both on individual and corporate level leadership will derive out of this virtue of a caring and sacrificing mother.

Supportive Brother

This term also derives from the root of a family concept and conveys an in-depth spiritual relationship. We find that this term is frequently used in the Bible. It shows kinship and ongoing and sustainable relationship. It points to solidarity and identification. Paul uses this term approximately thirty-five times in his epistles. He never got tired of telling his believers to encourage and exhort one another as brothers so that they remain steadfast in faith. It could also have been true of Paul himself in life and ministry; at times finding it hard to be alone in times such as hardships, loneliness, discouragement, hunger, tiring labour, misunderstanding, abuse and violation of rights and privileges without the mutual supportive fellowship of a brother.

Paul refers to Timothy as "our brother and God's servant" (1 Th. 3: 1); Epaphroditus as "my brother and fellow worker and fellow soldier" (Php. 2:25); and of Tychicus, Paul writes, "he is a beloved brother and faithful minister and fellow servant in the Lord" (Col. 4:7). Speaking about Onesimus, the apostle says: "The faithful and beloved brother, who is one of yourselves" (Col. 4:9). Paul not only was a supportive brother to these dear people, but also recognised his own need of them in the service of the Lord. This is a fitting style of identification with the followers, and they in turn will imitate the same principle in their leadership roles and development. This is an inner fortitude and freedom that seeks for the welfare and progress of those who have around and particularly of those brothers in Christ.

This reflects a sincere commitment that does not take advantage of the other (Matt. 12:48, 49; 1 Th. 4: 1; 1 John 3:16-18). Leaders that embody the role of a "supportive brother" identify themselves with those who minister, and they too may undergo vulnerable situations. In doing this, a leader keeps learning not only to receive, but also to give—this is sacrifice and sacrificial servant-hood (Matt. 7:3-8).

Watchful Shepherd

The portrait of a shepherd is a dominant form of leadership and a leadership role given in the Bible. In the Bible, Yahweh is described as the Shepherd of Israel (Ps. 23: 1- 4, 78:52; Micah 7:14; Zec. 9:16). Coming to the New Testament, Christ himself says, "I am the good shepherd (John10:14-16, 27). Although Pauline letters do not give us any direct reference to this term, undoubtedly, he too had a great sense of the shepherd-nature of his own ministry and clearly the ministry and development of any leader. The passage in Ephesians 4:11, 12, where "pastor" is mentioned as one of the spiritual gifts and the admonition of the apostle to the elders in Ephesus, substantiates this truth. Moreover, in Acts 20, the elders are identified as "overseers", which has a direct and literal reference to the role of a shepherd.

Leaders are shepherds of God's people, which mean they are the overseers. They serve with an unadulterated willingness and enthusiasm. Leaders as shepherds are not bosses but are to be examples. They ought to be good stewards of God's people—those who have been entrusted to us. The necessity and seriousness of the shepherding role is explained clearly in the following statement:

In order to be faithful shepherds, they first had to guard themselves. All leaders are vulnerable. We can be faithful. Satan will seek every opportunity to pounce on us and try to defeat us. So we must be vigilant. We must also protect God's people as this is part and parcel of our own role as overseers.[7]

Wise Elder

The role of an elder was so prominent in the Old Testament (Exod. 3:16, 24:1; Num. 11:25). Even today, this idea is not too alien, but is commonly used for referring to certain positions or ministries in the setting of a local church. Paul and Barnabas ordained "elders" in all the Asian churches (Acts 14:23). They were appointed after or with fasting and prayer. We learn that there were elders in the Church at Ephesus as cited in the farewell address of the apostle in Miletus. They are also called "overseers" in this passage (Acts 20:17-35). They hold a great task in that they are committed to watch over the people of God and are put into position by the Holy Spirit. They may have acted as a "presbytery" or council and must have had a prophetic ministry as well (1 Tim. 4:14). Paul told Titus to appoint "elders" in Crete. The elders are authorised to anoint the sick with oil and pray for healing (Jas.5:14). Elders are also mentioned as ones who preach and teach. Paul's advice to Timothy is that they are worthy of special honour (1 Tim. 5:17). The admonition of Peter to the elders is similar as well. He says that they ought to "tend the flock of God," overseeing the congregation (1 Pet. 5:2).

The idea of an elder holding a leadership function is vivid throughout Paul's writings. This function is vital to a group. A wise elder will be capable of entrusting and equipping more elders into various ministerial functions.

Obedient Servant

We have talked considerably about this aspect of the leadership role in the earlier chapters of the book. The title "servant of the

Lord" was a title of honour in the Old Testament (Exod. 4: 10; Ps. 119:17, 143:12). Servant Songs of Isaiah reveal a lot about the qualities of servant-hood. Jesus' ministry displays emphatically and expressly the servant character. He taught the disciples to be servants, that is, to serve the people and be "among" them (Mark 10:45: Matt. 20: 28; Luke 22:25-27; John 13: 3-5, 15-16). This is the pattern of the New Testament ministry of the Church. Paul frequently calls himself a servant—the bond slave of the Lord in the proclamation of the gospel (Rom. 1: 1; 2 Cor. 4:4; Gal. 1:10; Col. 4:12; 2 Pet. 1:1). This is quite opposite to the usual norm of leadership that we witness in the world. The leaders in the Church ought to be servants in every aspect of their leadership functions. Being a servant does not mean that we meet every demand and wish of the people but to meet their 'needs'—to be available to tend and feed them. In being servants does not mean to be at the biding of everybody but to be at the place where God wants one to be and serve him with complete obedience and faithfulness for the well-being of people.

Productive Manager

This may sound to be a very secular term to many of us. Surely so! Yet God wants leaders of His Church to be effective and productive wherever they are—by abiding in His word. It is an achiever model. The Lord has entrusted to the Church various gifts for its efficient and effective building up and growth. We have all the resources available and should properly utilise them in the ministry.

A leader as an effective manager will face varied challenges. He has to accept and shoulder new responsibilities, must take calculated risks and in the process encounter unexpected struggles and losses. The business of a pastor-leader is not to depend upon the size of the congregation, but to effectively employ what God has given, such as human resources, financial resources, abilities and talents and various gifts.

A leader in the role of a manager must have a strong sense of obligation and accountability. Leaders should be able to tell at the end of the day what they had done—the achievement. Only a person who has learned to be accountable will receive increased responsibility. It is true that we will make mistakes as we wrestle in the process of doing, but a leader will learn and grow through them. The parable of the talents provides a strong teaching and warning to us about this concept (Matt. 25:14-16; Luke 19:11-17).

Ourselves as Your Servants

The very word "minister" represents the Greek word *diakonos*, one of the words used for describing the servant Messiah in the New Testament. A careful study will make it apparently clear that the order of the New Testament ministry is described in terms of humble service. Paul always acknowledged that he and his group have an awesome pastoral relationship to their believers. This missionary group with Paul as its leader of the New Testament times is an equivalent to the ordained ministry of the Church today. Significantly, Paul describes this group as carrying out in some sense the work of the servants in the Church.

The book of Corinthians is a classic text in order to explore and substantiate this idea of the Apostle Paul. The gleanings from the few selected passages from the first and second books of Corinthians will help us understand the Pauline philosophy in the ministry. And, it is evident that the toils that he underwent in obedience to the call to be the servant of the Lord became the bedrock of everything that matured his philosophy and ministry. Thus, this discussion should lead us to a certain conclusion about who we are today, where we have failed and a biblical foresight into the future of our leadership.

Servants of Christ

In this lengthy passage (1 Cor. 3:18-4:13), Paul is dealing with a serious problem in the Corinthian church in relation to the leadership of the Church. He is approaching it by presenting to them that they (Apollos, Cephas and Paul) are all leaders of Corinthian believers. They are there for the purpose of serving them. Both the ministers and people belong to Christ (3:20-22). Paul was correcting the misconceptions and lack of discernment about those who are leaders—they are co-labourers with God. One of the reasons being they do not depend on people or their human wisdom (vs. 18-23). Servant leaders will never equate God's work or ministry belonging to a particular group, caste, colour, race, background or even to themselves. If they do, it will mean an immature attitude that operates merely on the human level, takes sides and shows partiality just as the world does (3:4).

Ministers are both the servants of Christ and the servants of the Church at the same time. A closer look at 1 Corinthians chapter 4 points to the same characteristics of Christ himself; mentioned as features identified by the apostle. The apostles are also like men sentenced to death as was Christ our Master. They are a spectacle to the world just as the Lord was made a spectacle to the world by carrying the cross to Golgotha. They are fools for the sake of Christ and are weak before the world; so also, the cross is seen as the "foolishness of God" and the "weakness of God." The apostles often faced hunger and thirst and were buffeted and homeless. So also was Christ during his earthly ministry. Bishop Yohannan writes:

> True Christian suffering comes because we live for God and are serving the expansion of His kingdom. It is a positive sacrifice for the good of others. It is not a morbid, introspective act that one does to oneself to feel or become spiritual."[8]

Servants will face suffering positively and victoriously for the sake of God's kingdom. The servants of God are specially chosen and equipped instruments to bring out divine purposes. Servants are only vehicles in the work of God. It is God who causes things to happen. He assigns and makes it grow. The servant attitude can only be developed when a leader acknowledges this dominant truth and becomes humble instrument in the hands of God, who causes all things. "All true building of the church, whether it includes starting a congregation or only continuing one already started, must be in perfect harmony with the one divine foundation which once laid by God, now lies forever."[9] Jesus Christ is the foundation, and a servant-leader builds on the same and never lays another, such as leaders who go astray from Jesus and make themselves the centre of focus. "Jesus' kingdom ministry is to be contained and extended as the church moves out in mission to the nations."[10]

We Faint Not: The Power of the Indwelling Christ

In this passage (2 Cor. 4:1-15), Paul elaborately speaks about the ministers as the ministers of the new covenant contrasting the ministry as a whole with that of Moses. He, as Moule says:

> ...dilates awhile upon the great phenomenon of the Christian ministry, its message, its motives, the divine energies which can alone sustain the minister, the illumination which his own spirit must needs receive if he is to shed the light of Christ around him.[11]

The ministers are slaves for Jesus' sake (v. 5). "Ourselves as your servants for Jesus' sake," was this great Christian worker's central and ultimate philosophy of the Christian ministry. It presents to us an idea not of magisterial but altogether ministerial. It is not only God desires to be so, because Jesus himself was the Servant first. The leaders serve the Church because Jesus serves the Church. The kingdom of God demands servant-hood to be a normative pattern. The servant, whether pastor, teacher, director, organisational head, or guide in things divine, has no ambition outside the glory of his or her heavenly Master.

The ministry he has received because of God's mercy, Paul disclaims for himself and for his companions any high standing or worthiness that might make them able and creditable of being placed in this ministry (v. 1). The sufficiency of the servant is *in* and *from* God. "We are not discouraged" is the declaration of the courage and optimism in view of the apparent failure and rejection of many towards the gospel. It also refers to the conduct of the Christian service, which is contrary to what secular offices often consider success. The assurance of the servants to succeed and not fail is because they participate in the ministry with and of God. Therefore, Paul says that "we are triumphant" (2:14), "we have confidence" (3:4) and "we faint not" (4:1, 16). Leaders are not lords over but helpers and coaches of people, and their joy is that they are "debtors to all for Christ's sake." Lenski clearly brings out the meaning of this portion:

> We are slaves who do nothing but serve Christ's people. Unselfishly, never complaining, seeking nothing, giving everything, listening to all allurements of threats, happy only when we heap up profit for others—so we slave... The very word 'Jesus' calls that here on earth...he came not to be ministered unto, but to minister, yea to give his life for many.[12]

Paul speaks of carrying around the "dying of Jesus" in his body (vs.10, 11). He says in detail what the suffering life in ministry involves in terms of Christ, the ministers and the Church. The phrase "being given up" in verse 11 and the phrase "he was betrayed" found in 1 Corinthians 11:23 are both the same root word in Greek, and it means as Hanson states; "...a reminder that the death of Jesus and the death-in-life of the ministers are equally part of God's plan. Finally, death-in-life and life through death are ultimately for the sake of the church."[13] Paul faced perilous hazards every hour and death every day (1Cor. 4:9; 15:30, 31). The death and life of Jesus were simultaneously evident in the experiences of the apostle Paul (1:4, 5). "It was not a matter of life after death, or even of life through death, but of life in the midst of death. Paul's repeated deliverances from occasions that led to death evidenced the resurrecting power of God...."[14] The suffering was part of the ministry of the apostle. Bishop Yohannan writes:

> This is a perfect example of the proper attitude toward suffering. It is never something we desire for its own sake, but something that we choose because it is necessary for the sake of the gospel... Instead he sues his suffering and sacrifice as the basis of his defence. Paul is saying that trials and tribulations authenticate, verify, and vindicate his ministry. To Paul suffering is the proof of his discipleship—not recognition or the symbols of success accepted by culture, society or even religious leaders.[15]

This rich theology of suffering was forged on the anvil of his own experience of the "suffering of Christ." We find, therefore, the concept of the servant central in the life of Christ, in the life of the ministry, in the life of the Church and in the Church's sacramental worship. As Glasser expounds:

> Indeed his theology of the Christian mission will stress suffering unavoidable, even essential to the sort of fruitful missionary service that "makes the word of God fully known" among the nations. From henceforth Paul will rejoice in his sufferings for the sake of the church.[16]

A Constraining Love

In this long section, Paul deals with the theme of the new covenant in the sphere of the ministry of reconciliation. Verses 14 and 15 interchangeably uses between Christ and Christians and recall the concept found in the passages of second Isaiah "...where the servant was both the people and the individual. Further, even when plainly the individual could only be meant, the individual was presented as acting on behalf of the people."[17] The ministry of the servant is judged or esteemed by Christ the Lord (5:10). Paul speaks about two motives for Christian service—knowledge of accountability to God (v.11) and the genuine consciousness of Christ's example of self-sacrificing devotion (v. 14). These verses teach two vivid truths. First of all, a follower of Christ is dead in Christ in order that all ambitions of carnal nature and longing for distinction and fame could be laid aside by the servant. Second, we owe to Christ our life and death because we are fully bonded to Himself. This brings one under the Lord's authority and makes his peculiar possession. No one must be reckoned as a servant of Christ on the ground of secular and/or external virtues and credibility of excellence, but on the pure inward qualities of Christ our Lord Himself.

God has reconciled the people to himself through Jesus Christ. He has also given the commission and authority to the ministers, whereby the servants are now the ministers of reconciliation and have been entrusted with the message of reconciliation for the people. Paul's vision of Jesus is not only just a character in history. It is a vision of faith with an eye of faith—the Messiah—Son of God—the Servant above all disguised by the very fact of the humble, lowly and unassuming status he had assumed. In this way, Jesus willingly identified himself with his own creation—the humans, that is, "taking the form of a man," he wrought about reconciliation. This means that he not only gladly served the people, but also embraced and carried out the awesome task of reconciling them to God through his life of submission and the voluntary death on the cross. The apostle affirms thrice that the ministry is given to us by God (vs. 18, 19). This ministry is not confined to the so-called ordained ministers according to Saint Paul. This activity of Christ, the supreme Servant, is taken up by the Church and the ministers and is lived so vividly in the life of humans, people outside Christ.

In the view of the Apostle Paul, the sufferings and hardships that accompany the ministry are not at all vague. In the sixth chapter, Paul drives home the idea of the life of Christ and that of the ministers on an equal plane. Christ the Servant had everything; as having nothing, he gave up everything to the point of a criminal and condemned personality of a servant. But this gained the victory for the Servant, which made him the Lord of all.

Insights and Applications

The exposition of these passages should have familiarised us to a certain degree with the philosophy of Paul in ministry and how earnestly he strove and laboured to imitate Christ and integrate the servant-attitudes in serving the Master. This is normal to any leadership expected of by our Lord, even today. Nothing less than that! In order for one to become useful for God in service to the Church and society, these principles are a must followed with wholehearted and sincere enthusiasm. Hanson's statement is an apt conclusion to this:

> Thus it is clear that if the ministers are to be servants of the Servant, then the church as a whole must be a servant also. The ministry is not independent of the church of the Servant.... The Servant Messiah carries out his ministry in the lives of his ministers. His life is reproduced in their lives, so they also are servants. But this ministry is exercised in and towards the church, so as to enable the church itself to carry out the ministry of the Servant. The Messiah came as a Servant; his ministers are servants, and the church he created is a Servant-church.[18]

Leader and Ministry of Reconciliation

The absolute foundation to and of reconciliation is the activity of God through Christ's death on the cross. This death that was a sacrifice, propitiatory suffering that was on behalf of humankind (1 Cor. 5:7; Rom. 3:25; 5:9, 10). It was the spontaneous nature and expression of God himself. The death of Christ was "on behalf of the people of the world." The simple yet noble element should stimulate us in our endeavour to be sold out for the sake of the community we represent. The very term 'reconciliation' "originates from the societal sphere (1 Cor. 7: 11) and speaks in general of the restoration of right relationship between two parties, placed often against enmity and alienation and positively peace."[19] The ministry of reconciliation means reconciling or mending broken relationships between people and restoring them to friendship. The passage in Ephesians 2:13-16 denotes that human beings are divided against one another at their core with varying combinations of race, language, colour, religion, educational status, job status and family status. These differences can find their solutions only in the "once for all accomplished work of Christ" on the cross, whereby he has broken down these dividing walls and has spelled out peace to us. In this, he has also shown to us the model of a new society by "creating a new being" from both the Jews and the Gentiles (that is, today, the whole world of people), in which no dividing complexion finds its place and value.

Forgiveness

The theory of reconciliation comes into actuality and experience only in terms of repentance by the wrongdoer and forgiveness by the one sinned against. There is a great amount of initiation on the part of God in terms of forgiveness, for it is he who has to forgive and give us the ability to forgive others. "The message of the cross is a message of free and unconditional forgiveness, although on man's side it required repentance."[20] Reconciliation, that is, forgiveness is so spontaneous on the part of God, for his character is to forgive and forgive abundantly, but repentance and obedience are expected on the part of human beings. In other words, "For what is forgiveness but reconciliation on the basis of righteousness and truth?

Forgiveness is the restoration of a personal relationship whether between people or between human beings and God."[21]

In the ministry and work of reconciliation, true forgiveness is experienced in spite of any consideration to who is right or wrong or best. The ministers pass on the grace of God to fellow believers and workers through their life and activity.

Agape Love

The very act of reconciliation itself is founded on love. This is to say that restoration of a broken relationship or fellowship is possible only by unfailing and unselfish demonstration of love. The love that has overflowed from Jesus is a call to reconciliation for all peoples, but with humility and repentance (Rom. 5:10). The central motive of reconciliatory work is love and only love, and it is love "in spite of." Ladd wrote:

> Reconciliation is an act of God, initiated by his love, by virtue of which God no longer counts trespasses against them. It has to do with divine attitude toward men as the result of which God no longer looks upon them as enemies and as hostile.[22]

The statement of Gilliland is noticeable in this regard. How Paul's injunctions of love stands out! They cover all attitudes, judge all motives and guard every action. The individual Christian is to learn love because he has been changed by love. Each Christian is to be the servant of each other in love (Gal. 5:13).[23]

True Christian love is the fundamental rule in an attitude of tolerance. Prominent in the discussions leading to reconciliation was the injunction of Romans 14:13: "Never do anything that would make your fellow believer stumble or fall into sin."[24]

The guiding factor for us as leaders should be the words of Jesus himself: "A new commandment I give to you, that you love one another" (John 13:34). And, as Peter says, "above all hold unfailing love for one another, since love covers a multitude of sins" (1Pet. 4:8). Scott writes, "If the *koinonia* of the church is the *koinonia* of the Spirit, it is also and will be the *koinonia* of agape."[25]

Fellowship

Only two persons who agree with each other can have fellowship. Someone defined fellowship the following way: "Two fellows in the same boat." Yet the Christian fellowship is one that involves all diversities, but diversity in unity. Why? Because the focus is not on diversity but unity; and that is unity in love, in the bond of fellowship in and through the Son Jesus Christ and in the power of the Holy Spirit. In the first resort, our fellowship is with God the Father, the Son and the Holy Spirit. But it is an extended fellowship and, in fact, is made a reality only when those who have fellowship with one another on the basis of the divine principles of reconciliation.

Fellowship Is Reconciliation

This is a relationship with one another in the Body in which each member functions mutually, cordially and united in bringing reconciliation to all aspects of the Body-life. By this, they demonstrate the ministry of reconciliation both within and outside the Body, the Church. The concept of fellowship mentioned in the Bible is not with the pet group that one likes or with people whom one likes the most; it is one that embraces diversities—all communities, cultures, languages, nations and peoples. Indeed it is one of the tests in leadership. The ability and vision to make everyone perfect and treat as equal before God is the principle for liberating and unleashing the full potential of each person as heirs in Christ. It is a great responsibility and a great task. God's call is a call to bonded love-fellowship. That is, the supreme value of life is friendship against the supreme horror of life, which is loneliness. Just note this gentle statement of Jesus Christ: "Greater love has no one than this, that one lay down his life for his friends..." (John 15:13-14).

Thinking Further in this Regard

First, how often do we take the initiative and risk in introducing young, fresh and emerging, but new leadership potential? Ananias is a typical example of the kind of leader who shrinks, pulls back and shies away from taking initiative. He said, "Lord, I have heard from many about this man, how much evil he has done to thy saints at Jerusalem..." (Acts 9:13, 14). It was natural, honest and justifiable for Ananias to think in that way. It was also true on the part of the people at Damascus (Acts 9:21). But we need leaders like Barnabas (son of encouragement) who will provide a pulpit—an emerging context for a young leader. We need the gift of godly discernment and unselfishness to do so. Do we keep upcoming leaders from emerging by being overly critical? Although certain amount of evaluation is necessary to help the process, we should not hinder the free progress and growth of an emerging leader.

Second, what are the kinds of suffering and hardships generally faced by leaders? Paul has encountered both the internal and the unseen—the mental, emotional and physical sufferings in the task of his mission. Even in such awful situations, he had maintained a sense of integrity, inseparable loyalty, optimism and faith. How committed are leaders today when faced with hardships? Are we compromising or are purity and truth girding our life? To what extent is our commitment and dedication true in the face of a complex situation? Are we presenting Jesus, the pure Gospel, or are we propagating a 'different' gospel? Or are we trying mixed and indirect means and thus losing the effectiveness, quality and greatness of the Gospel?

Third, we must give consideration to the various roles and functions of leadership situations. How competent are the leaders—the pastors, heads of various institutions or departments of the Church of our day in teaching the word of God? I am not talking just of compatibility in line with a logical, systematic, apologetic and rationalistic or argumentative level of development and gathering of information in presenting the Gospel. And I am also not talking just in line with administrative and managerial skills and compatibility. At the same time, it is not my point to ignore them. With all due respect to such homiletic skilfulness for defining and presenting the Scripture, a leader should also be able to practically expound it from the application point of view. Lack of "head knowledge" is not our problem today.

The ability to "rightly dividing the word of truth", pure and unadulterated teaching, and expounding God's word—not coloured with one's own story of success but allowing the Bible to expound, exegete and expound itself—is the key. Not using attractive stories or illustrations to fit into a point being made or a point one wants to make often may not be the way the Spirit would want to communicate. Often communication takes place, but lacks the power since the Spirit is not backing it up. A spiritual seed needs to grow, and that can only happen when the Spirit of God is there; not just in our eloquent and persuasive ways of fitting in examples and stories that may add flavour but miss the divine life. We should, therefore, be very careful to use proven examples. Jesus has spoken things of eternity using parables, but he has used or picked all or most of them from nature and daily life of people and situations: not of persons themselves. Surprisingly, if he used examples of persons it was mostly of negative attribute and character used as an example of warning to others in order to refrain from. If the Lord has used, it was when proven with constancy and quality—not only activities and performance based but of proven and sustained character.

The issue is how competent are those principles lived in daily life? Do leaders zealously practice what is preached and taught? Are the existing leaders producing and developing future leadership that will learn and imitate the godly patterns from them? If a leader is competent in "doing" what is preached, the emerging and young leaders will have a great future. How much of the "guru-sishya" model of our cultural and religious system could be appropriated today in our quest for training and developing future leaders? Deep and creative thoughts must be given to this area.

Fourth, how are our behaviour, conduct and life lived among ourselves? This is another issue to evaluate. Are we supportive, sacrificial and fatherly in our behaviour both in regard to position and followers? How much of a shepherding nature and lifestyle do we reflect in ministry? What amount of compassion and care is demonstrated in leadership to the flock or to those whom God has entrusted to the care? How active is personal witnessing and involvement of leaders in the mission of the Lord? Do disputes, divisions and discord prevail among leaders due to ungodly desires in the functions of leadership? The attitudes of unaccountability and unfaithfulness are issues that require a thorough straightening and purifying work of the Spirit. A great hindrance to the task of proclamation and testimony today is division and partisan spirit among leaders themselves and in the Church at large. This takes root due to lack of mutual thinking and co-operation among leaders in the larger vision of the mission and building up of God's kingdom. Nonetheless, to say that leaders as shepherds are the key for revival, revitalisation and blessings as we read in the book of Ezekiel chapter 22. And, this area of life and mission must be at once put through a real searching of the Holy Spirit.

Fifth, how can those who are looking for integrity, solidarity and meaning in life find Jesus as the Way if they keep bolstering the "wall" of denominations? Many people do not find Christianity different from their own religion as they also face issues such as casteism and different branches of belief and "denominations." This is not in reference to the varied forms of ecumenical movements we have today. They are needed and important. But a majority of them are so-called entities that merely place themselves on the superficial and surface level of Christian witness and experience. My contention is that we have to provide a way for people to experience solidarity, security and identity that they can have in Christ. This is possible only when we willingly throw away all the external barriers and become united, practice fellowship and live a life patterned after love and fellowship. This should first begin among the leaders and move on to the people we serve. This indeed is servant-leadership! This is normal Christian leadership as we see in the Holy Bible. This is the service of the servant-leader.

Paul has so much to teach us about leadership. He was always "spending out" for the people whom he served for the cause of the Kingdom of God. Let each one of us be willing and obedient and humbly consider each one as servant of the Lord. The ministry of reconciliation means to live in one brotherhood in spite of divisions and differences; not in total absence of disagreements and differences, but mutual respect for one another. Leaders are the instruments, agents and organisms through which the purpose and plan of God in Jesus Christ must be carried out. Let each one be passionate about bringing every tribe, people and race to reconciliation and about enabling them to be, in turn, ministers of the same truth. It is possible only when God's leaders—those in leadership of His Church—"do nothing from selfishness or conceit, but in humility count others better than themselves" (Php. 2:3).

Endnotes

[1] Greenslade, *op. cit.*, pp. 163-165

[2] Richards, *op. cit.*, p. 25.

[3] *Ibid.*, p. 131.

[4] *Ibid.*, p. 134.

[5] Greenslade, *op. cit.*, p. 131.

[6] *Ibid.*, p. 133.

[7] Chua Wee Hian, *The Making of a Christian Leader*, Downers Grove: Inter Varsity Press, 1987, p. 44.

[8] Yohannan, *op. cit.*, p. 68.

[9] R. C. H. Lenski, *The Interpretation of First and Second Corinthians*, Minnesota: Augsburg Publishing House, 1963, p. 135.

[10] Glasser, *op. cit.*, p. 33.

[11] Handley C. G. Moule, *The Second Epistle to the Corinthians*, Chicago: Moody Press, 1962, p. 26.

[12] Lenski, *op. cit.*, p. 967.

[13] Hanson, *op. cit.*, pp. 51-52.

[14] Frank E. Gaeblain (Ed.), *The Expositors Bible Commentary*, Grand Rapids: Zondervan Publishing House, 1976, p. 343.

[15] Yohannan, *op. cit.*, p. 69.

[16] Glasser, *op. cit.*, p. 130.

[17] Hanson, *op.cit.*, p. 55.

[18] Hanson, *op. cit*, pp. 59-60.

[19] Herman Ridderbos, *Paul: An Outline of his Theology*, Grand Rapids: W.B. Eerdmans, 1975, p. 182.

[20] Charles Anderson Scott, *Christianity According to St. Paid*, Cambridge: University Press, 1927, p. 83

[21] John Knox, *Chapters in a life of Paid*, New York: Abingdon, 1950, p. 146.

[22] G. E. Ladd, *The Gospel of the Kingdom*, Grand Rapids: W. B. Eerdmans Co., 1986, p. 453.

[23] Dean S. Gilliland, *Pauline Theology and Mission Practice*. Grand Rapids: Baker Book House, 1983, pp. 130.

[24] *Ibid.*, pp. 158-59.

[25] Charles Anderson Scott, *op. cit.*, p. 139.

Chapter 5

Leadership for Tomorrow

Holistic Christian ministry and leadership are built on relationships. They are not built on programmes, finances, status, position and fame, technology, plans or methods. Leadership is a vital need of churches today, but it begins with God and people and culminates in God for the people. It is ultimately based on trust, encouragement, love and development of people based on reconciliation resulting in hope and transformed lives.

Building Trusting Relationships

God began his work by building relationships with humans; so also leaders must begin by developing proper relationships with individuals and group to and for which they minister. In order to bring us to God, Christ lived among us and served us; so also leaders must incarnate Christ in all aspects of their ministry.

Leadership is, therefore, the continuation and extension of Christ in the world—those who are broken and suffering; in order to bring them to God and to train, develop and mature them in the image of Christ. Building relationships, however, is not an easy task for any leader. More particularly, when there are wrong motives, attitudes and lack of co-operation within the group itself. Here comes the real test for leaders; unless a leader is in the job because of a personal call from the Lord and his appointment, the result could be one of defeat and/or trying to do things in the flesh. Leaders need special anointing and grace to prove themselves in times of such testing.

Relationships of mutual understanding and trust are the foundation on which all leadership training, development and ministries must be built. Without this leaders are aliens and the phases of formation and development programme merely a foreign import. We often label people according to how they look or their behaviour, or even their origins and relate to them based on these labels. We create 'blocks' in our relationships. We ignore their beauty, capabilities and strengths and more importantly, what they can offer. Healthy relationships are prevented because of these labels.

Relationships need to be carefully cultivated, fostered and maintained throughout life and ministry of the leader. There are many blocks or barriers in building and rebuilding a healthy and trusted relationship and experiencing and advancing the graces. This we need to overcome.

Premature Judgements

The judgmental attitude towards people with a preoccupied and prejudiced mind could be one of the many obstacles that need to be confronted. Prejudice is a natural human inclination. This occurs particularly when we judge people without ample knowledge and information of the facts, context and an honest understanding of the individual. Too often we judge people based on their background, such as caste, race, economical standings and education. Too often we judge people before having understood the situation at hand. At times, we do not appreciate the abilities and strengths merely because of selfish and personal bias, interests and agendas. It can make individuals and ministries ineffective. Leaders should learn to appreciate people and build healthy relationships. Relationships should take priority over the tasks; people are more important than the task itself.

Ethnocentrism

The second barrier could be that of ethnocentrism. This is a high-minded feeling that what one does, thinks or plans is better than the ideas and plans of those with whom one serves and works. This is serious a barrier to building up a successful relationship and effective leadership. One may just pay "lip-service" to what others say and to their contributions. This feeling of supremacy in leaders over others invariably has an adverse effect on the growth, function and development of people and ministry. It is not to suggest that leaders must not be sharp in thinking and planning, but they should stay away from having a sense of superiority over others. People are quick to notice this sense of superiority in leaders and when they sense it they become suspicious of them and distance themselves from them. Sincere appreciation of people and their gifting are vital in building trusted and stable relationships. This is possible only when leaders begin to consider them as their equal.

Misunderstanding

This element can totally paralyse the efficiency and morale of an organisation or ministry. It can cause serious damage to ministries and people. Therefore, leaders need to be extremely careful about how they respond to the information they receive from people and other sources and how they ultimately judge others. Only proper understanding can remove misunderstanding. Leaders must, therefore, try to get as much information about the matter at hand as possible and carefully examine it before forming an opinion or passing a judgement. As shepherds their job is not to expose but to protect, guard and develop the followers and lead them to greater avenues and spheres.

Sharing the Ministry

In leadership training and development, leaders should share the work, control, pulpit, vision, and achievements with others to benefit all. God has commissioned leaders to reveal Himself through the corporate life of His own people to a world that does not know Him. Fighting and power struggles among leaders certainly bring dishonour to God. Leaders have to embody the Church, the "people of God", and should teach and train believers in the light of this awesome truth. Our feeling of independence must be broken in order to build a community that will exercise and mobilise its gifts. There ought to be mutual confession and true love for one another. Michael Green says that "the effectiveness of our ministry depends upon the fervency of our love and affection for one another."[1]

Delegating Community Concerns

The leadership functions and gifts in the Body of Christ are for providing the help that is needed for each Christian to understand and recognise his or her place, purpose and importance in this body. The task of the leader is that of "equipping the saints" at least in two ways. The saints are for the "work of ministry" and "building up of the Body" towards "mature manhood" and for manifesting the spiritual gifts in these realms (Eph. 4: 11-13). And its basis is the Word of God. Leaders of our day, therefore, need to gain an insight into leadership as a shared exercise of spiritual gifts by each member of the local church, institution and organisation and mobilise the community to that effect. The work of ministry will never be properly and effectively accomplished by a weak and unhealthy church, torn with internal pains and ruined by spiritual diseases. "The leaders first give the followers a job, and then let them do it. All too often a leader will delegate a job, and then meddle and fuss to the point where he has actually taken the task away from the person. This is a classic mistake."[2] The whole community grows up together into maturity and fullness when each member of the Body ministers according to the gifting.

The leader being the key to experiencing growth should have a correct understanding of the church as the building of God. This illustrates the importance of unity. Instead of creating or widening the breach, leaders should have the wisdom of dealing with differences that create disharmony. Church disciplines are very important, but they must be exercised with a redemptive attitude and in love. Leaders need to acknowledge the fact that the future of the Church and society depends upon unity and love—a healthy and wholesome community, which alone is the basis of a wholehearted and life-long commitment.

Servant-leaders are obliged to keep moral purity, religious integrity and love (Eph.5:22, 23; 2 Cor. 11:2, 3; Rev.2: 1-7). The call is not only to be the bride faithful but also the bride in love. Leaders should have complete allegiance to the Lord and to people so that Christian growth and maturity are promoted. Such a leadership function, which is in turn passed on to the members, will be winsome, forgiving, compassionate and attractive.

Servant-leaders are on the battlefront and serve to mobilise the army of God, the Church, to fight against Satan and the evils in society. Three vital elements of this need to be remembered in this regard: The enemy, the leader and the whole armour of God. The enemy should be spotted—the world, the flesh and the devil. Leaders should always be reminded that Satan is trying to seduce us and the believers with the free offering of worldly attractions (1 John 2:15, 16). How great the situation would have been today if we had rightly spotted the enemy and fought against him as a united and committed army of God! Instead of fighting the enemy, we end up fighting against one another—thanks to Satan's hard work.

Mobilising the Total Gifting

Christ the Victor is our leader. He is the "Captain of our salvation." Leaders are those who trust the Lord fully and direct the Body to be submissive and obedient to Him and to those in authority over them. Leaders must turn their minds towards Jesus. This calls for maintaining right relation-ships in every area and love and submission to one another.

A Christian leader should work hard to foster harmonious relationships in community and society and respect for other faiths. Love and service should be the guiding principle in all relationships.

The highest responsibility of a leader is to train followers and unite them in order to strive together against the wiles of the devil and to equip people to fight both individual and corporate battles. Leaders must learn to put aside even the harmless and good pursuits that may in any way hinder training and effectiveness. The equipping must thoroughly be disciplined as soldiers in the army of God (Eph.6:10-18; Heb. 12:1-3). No conflicts or divisions in the body can win a battle; only a strong, united, disciplined and trained unit can win a battle when mobilised. Unfortunately, most of today's leadership—be it the Church or the nation—has deviated from facing the true enemy. Satan has done all kinds of damage. He has defeated us to a great extent. Only an honest realisation of our failure and a thorough removal of our spiritual haughtiness and narrow-mindedness in the light of the Lord can lead us to victory.

Transformed Community of Disciples

The Church should be equipped for ministry to itself and to the world through the empowerment of spiritual gifting. Leaders are the means to achieving this end through the working of the Holy Spirit. The equipping of the Church must be wholesomely displayed in a lifestyle of obedience and discipleship. The unique call of the leader in the Body is commitment to discipling. Leaders are called by Jesus—this is a call to obedience, service, simple lifestyle and caring for the poor, the unwanted, the rejected and the 'nobodies' in society. It is a life that revolves around the Master characterised by sacrifice and servant-hood—willing servants. Leaders are called to multiply; they must strive to build effective leadership for the future. This is possible only by "being" an example.

This means that leaders are called to be an extension and continuation of Jesus in this world. They must strive to enable the redeemed individuals to follow in the footsteps of Jesus Christ—to emulate Jesus in their everyday lives. This is living the 'identification principle'—emulating the life of the leader and being available and one among them. The fact is that "a leader should be a friend who is there in time of need."[3]

Leaders must assure committed leadership. Leadership is discovered and founded on submission and humility. There is power in submission and "fellowship." Leadership in the Church means submission to and friendship with Christ. True submission facilitates love and peace. Jesus' authority came forth from his submission to the Father. So also a leader should derive authority in speech and action because of their submission to Christ and to one another. Such leaders will have a God-given vision, which they will pass on to the faithful.

Servant-leaders will stir up spiritual gifts in others. Wagner says that "well mobilized laity is a sign of a healthy church."[4] This is possible only when we help them discover their gifts, motivate them to exercise their gifts, facilitate structures that will give them a platform to be active and productive and guide them into meaningful avenues of service in and to their community. Servant-leaders must carefully and prayerfully involve in multiplying lay leaders and leading them to a holistic ministry with opportunity and avenues to exercise their gifts. Clear priorities must be established to encourage others to do the Kingdom mandate of proclaiming the good news to the poor and needy.

Servant-leaders should, without fail, foster the development of dynamic leaders. They should continue in the ministry by extending vision, power, strategies, stability and model for future leadership. They should always mobilise the spiritual gifts of the laity as a principal factor in training, developing and establishing a dynamic base for church leadership. This way they can develop a ministry team in each of the local congregations. This is essential to our ministry and a strong means to leadership training, community development and church growth.

Servant-leaders are committed stewards in terms of their finances, time, talents, friendships, service and the people entrusted to them. These are important aspects for training lay people and young leaders as well. They have a vital and undisputed role in the leadership of the Church. In fact, our call is to be servants of the Servant and serve him and his people. Let us be ardent, immovable, exemplary and life-giving leaders. Let us serve him with gladness and create a people, especially leaders, who will manifest in themselves, in the church, and in its service the life and "being" of Jesus Christ himself.

Power of Listening

Listening well leads to better relationships. Good or bad relationships among the peers have a direct impact on a person and an organisation's bottom line. Miscommunication hurts our life and organisations by lowering people's morale, productivity and resourcefulness.

In today's world, we depend too heavily on e-mail, blackberry, text messaging, telephone, video conferencing, social medias and the like; we have forgotten the art of face-to-face encounter. All these modern facilities are useful and must be used. But personal and interpersonal communication, coaching, mentoring and one-on-one guiding cannot be replaced for developing leadership.

"The ear of the leader must ring with the voices of the people", said Woodrow Wilson, a former president of America. God has given us two ears but only one mouth! It has an unequivocal practical insight integrated within. Responding rightly and effectively requires an inbuilt ability—the ingredients of feelings and emotions. Humans are made of these two fundamental elements and respond mostly and often based on these stimuli. It is only through active listening that one can develop this skill and, thereby, an active relationship. Patience, openness, discernment and fervour for understanding are required to develop this skill.

"In some South Pacific cultures, a speaker holds a conch shell as a symbol of temporary position of authority. Leaders must understand who holds the conch—that is, who should be listened to when," says Max De Pree. A leader is one who has a genuine interest in others—the needs of others—the voice of others. A leader should know both personal and corporate needs both of followers and leaders, co-workers and the larger community. A listening ear must be developed for the needs of people and practiced in sharing. It is possible only when one sincerely intends to listen and understand in the rein of thoughts of the other. Willingness to listen that disturbs and discomforts, eagerness to obtain grass-roots realities from the bottom-line, accessing lower-level people and not just one or two whom one may 'like' or use to feed in alone will not help in listening to the voice from below. Genuine leaders respond correctly and creatively to such situations.

"Effective listeners remember that 'words have no meaning—people have meaning.' The assignment of meaning to a term is an internal process; meaning comes from inside. And although our experiences, knowledge and attitudes differ, we often misinterpret each other's message while under the illusion that a common understanding has been achieved," says Larry Barker. Stepping into the shoe of others, entering into another's pain and trying to empathetically understand—sincerely understand—the other are the qualities of an able leader. It points towards leading with pure and deeper ability of discernment—of people, co-workers and the emerging leaders. Disposition of a mature mind and attitude are the qualities that allow a leader to listen patiently. The biblical principle, "Quick to listen and slow to speak" is an imperative skill in any leadership lifestyle (Ref. Jas. 1:19). This serves to build up relationships and thereby leads to finding solutions to grave problems.

"You have to be willing sometime to listen to some remarkable bad opinions. Because if you say to someone, 'That's the silliest thing I've ever heard, get on out here'—then you'll never get anything out of that person again, and you might as well have a puppet on a string or a robot," says John Bryan. Becoming an active and dynamic listener is the key in this process. It requires and calls for a commitment to time and vigour. Discovering present skills and taking adequate steps towards improving those skills are valuable gestures for improving leadership and communication skills. Good leaders identify and deal with those distractions and deal with them; they are focused in purpose. Notwithstanding, they listen with the intention of helping the person and facing the emerging situation and challenge.

The Iron Rod and the Whip
The leader is not meant to be an arbiter, a ruling autocrat, a power-exercising person. In Christ, those who lead have authority—moral and spiritual authority and power earned through Christ-like nature over those whom they lead. It is not 'forced upon' or exercised with the 'rod and whip' style. Authority should never be exercised as though people were slaves or suppressed beings. However, it also does not mean that there should not be any control. Ultimately, leaders are called to LEAD, not to condemn and pass premature judgments.

The leader must be a 'one-integrated-personality' in approach, method, style, relationship and planning both within and outside. The true and genuine leadership style is open, sincere, transparent and unblemished and seeks the good of others in thoughts, motives and purpose—even in the subconscious mind. An effective leadership style passes on skills, intelligence and experience to young and emerging leaders.

Judgmental, prejudicial and indifferent attitude and conduct—singling out individuals based on likes and dislikes of a person, preventing one from emerging and becoming established and so on—should not figure in leadership. This is the 'iron rod and whip' style of leadership. Instead, leadership should be based on mercy, compassion, empathy, concern for others, mutual respect and so on. The simple rule is that people are more important than 'activity' and 'project.'

The common and natural tendency is to focus on one's failings. The way of Jesus was totally different. The Bible admonishes us to reinstate and establish—with a spirit of humility and lowliness—those who fail and sin. Jesus pointed out people's failings, but He did that to re-establish them to the fullness of life and activities.

It is the obligation and duty of an existing and older leader to strengthen those who are weak. It is the pre-eminent virtue of a good leader. A weak link in a chain should be strengthened and put right, not discarded; for if it is discarded, the chain will be of no use. Look for what is still left in the 'weak' person— the thing that can be strengthened and used for God's Kingdom. See the rule stated in the Holy Bible: "A bruised reed he will not break, and a smoldering wick he will not snuff out" (Isa. 42: 3, Matt. 12:20). Giving hope to the weak and failing ones is the golden way. A loving and caring relationship and humility-based on loving and firm correction and guidance to show the way and give impetus to greater growth are the foundational call and commitment required of a leader. This is what the Apostle Paul meant when he wrote: "Do not lay hands upon anyone too hastily and thereby share responsibility for the sins of others; keep yourself free from sin." In another version, it says do not be hasty in laying on of hands on a "young convert" (1Tim. 5: 22). A person should be given time and context to grow and to 'emerge.'

The call is for a single-minded goal, which can be achieved if the elderly and existing leaders and the young and emerging ones move along with one desire and aim. The focus should be more on upholding individuals, dignity, honour, development and growth than on victories and failures, personal interest and achievements.

Forget not the Beginning
When we think of leadership for tomorrow, we need to look at how we got to where *we are now*. To find this out, we need to ask a few simple questions: Where did I start? What was my beginning? What were the early stages and experiences of the

life I lived? What were the situations, people and circumstances in the various stages of my growing up? Who were the persons who held on to me and took interest in guiding me through? What position did I occupy before I got to the current leadership position? If we look back, we will in all probability realise that everything came from God's will and grace. This realisation will surely lead us into greater humility, brokenness, godly fear and reverence—the things that led us into assuming our current duties.

"Do not despise the day of small beginnings" (Zech. 4:10), for God is in those beginnings. God delights in taking the insignificant and making something out of it. Down through history we see this divine pattern. Never despise your "small beginnings." Look at them in the light of the Lord and say: "Not by might, not by power, but my Spirit, says the Lord Almighty" (Zech. 4:6; 1 Cor. 1:26-29). God the Creator knows everything and can change the course of one's life. We need to honour God by our continued surrender in His presence.

A wise person should not put his trust in his wisdom, and a weak person in his weakness. Both must submit humbly to the Lord, who builds and shapes lives in accordance with His supernatural design. Since God develops future leaders, we should simply submit to God's will.

Others Are not a Threat
Those who have been redeemed by the blood of Jesus Christ are members of the body of Christ—the Church. According to the Apostle Paul, the children of God make up the members of the Church. Every member's life is unique—his or her life situation, morale, occupation, works and so on. At the same time, we are one body in Christ.

If it is so, existing leaders should not feel threatened by emerging leaders—leaders who may seem to be more capable, more skillful and more zealous about their commitment and call. Comparison in this regard is not called for. Instead, existing leaders should contribute fully towards the emergence and growth of young leaders. "Looking unto Jesus, the author and perfector of our faith" (Heb. 12:2)—this is the source and fountain of all energy and resources. He enlarges, equips and perfects both existing and emerging leaders in accordance with individual vision and commitment.

How do we arrive at such a wholesome state of mind and revelation? What are the fundamental ingredients of such a life attitude? As I see, they are: the absolute assurance of call and personal involvement in the Kingdom's work, a genuine personal understanding of strengths and weaknesses and a personal involvement in the larger work and service of the Church. This life attitude is born out of deliberate willingness and submission and remains rooted in absolute contentment. Look at the great statement of the Apostle Paul in 1 Corinthians, chapter 3: 6-7: "I planted the seed, Apollos watered, but it is God who gives the increase..." Only such a leader can rejoice in working for God's Kingdom. This is the kind of leadership that God wants to see—leaders who fulfil the entrusted responsibility without threat and fear.

Delegation with Freedom and Empowerment
What is delegation? Delegation means the process of giving someone work or responsibilities that would usually be yours.

Each leadership style is situational. It depends heavily on the task, the team or individual's capabilities and knowledge, the time and tools available and the results desired. It very much depends on 'the tell, sell, consult, join and delegate' model and style.

The older leaders should foster the younger and emerging ones. This will enable the members of the team to put their best feet forward and ensure progressive growth and development as leaders. Successful delegation gives confidence, authority and empowerment and ensures that a leader is matured and groomed for the future. This enhances the morale of the institution.

It is common knowledge that delegation without empowerment is no delegation at all. The elements of proper delegation are as follows: Each person will have the freedom to think independently; voice their opinions and suggestions in a forum or group; fair amount of provision and space for sharing opinions, incorporating and implementing those that are workable, practical and creative; and measurable authority, responsibility and accountability. The existing leader must have the vision to "fan into flame" new and creative opinions rather than pouring "cold water" on them. Interfering after having delegated responsibility is not actual and genuine delegation. This type of involvement will nullify the confidence of the other. When a delegation is made, it must be done with a fair amount of freedom and empowerment. Style and method may differ, but principles stay on.

Usually, the existing leader feels that only he or she knows how to handle a process and that the younger leader is incompetent and does not have a proper understanding of the process in question. Such a leader becomes over-enthusiastic and in his or her desire to ensure that things are done the way the existing leader expects, he or she ends up thwarting the life-giving vision of the younger leader.

Existing leaders should not think of exercising 'absolute' power or authority over younger leaders. However, when their involvement becomes necessary, they must lead the process creatively, skillfully, judiciously and intelligently. This will keep the younger leader's focus and vision intact. Consider, for example, Moses' appointment of the seventy elders under him to help in leadership. Moses, leading the people of Israel and journeying towards the Promised Land, found himself working hard from early morning till late night to resolve the countless conflicts that arose among his people. He had become a workaholic—probably unintentionally. When Moses' father-in-law saw the unsustainable workload and realised that Moses was heading for trouble, he pulled Moses aside and became the leadership consultant and he the client. At least five invaluable principles of delegation and empowerment can be spotted in the Bible (Ref. Exod. 18:1-26).

Complete Dependence on God

A spiritual leader always depends on God. The most important spiritual lesson to learn while walking with God is what God has taught His children—the people of Israel in the wilderness: Humans do not live on bread alone but on every word that comes from the mouth of God (Deut. 8:1-5). This is a lesson both the existing and younger leaders must continually learn and relearn—complete dependence on God.

This dependence or trust is much deeper and stronger than saying 'I believe' and 'I trust.' This disposition of mind will reduce self, pride and selfish desires to dust; Christ and His will permeate all aspects of life and one yields to God completely. It is at this moment that we reach the highest and glorious spiritual experience of confessing "it is no more I; but Christ lives" (Ref. Gal. 3:1-3).

Such an experience reveals leadership qualities. The words of Jesus, "Take my yoke and learn of me" (Matt. 11: 29), and those of Saint Paul, "As I follow Christ, you be imitators of me" (1 Cor. 11:1) highlight the kind of attitude that leaders must have. This attitude in an existing and older leader goes a long way towards inspiring a younger and emerging leader.

Leadership entails loyalty to God; a leader is willing to forgo personal wishes and desires while serving the Lord. Take a look at what the Apostle Paul says about his life and ministry in 2 Corinthians 3:5. He declares that "not that of ourselves we are competent to decide anything by our own reasoning, but our competency comes from God..." Only an absolute and resolute commitment to God and a total dependence on Him can usher in strong and unshakable leadership of tomorrow.

Lifestyle of Service
The fruitfulness and influence of leadership are measured by how much of service-mindedness one has. Service is not the language of title, position and power but of love and action. In other words, failures and mistakes should become stepping stones to greater power and increased vision.

The leadership style of Lord Jesus Christ was based on humility, love and gentleness. One who wishes to be first, be first the servant –this was the rule and philosophy of our Lord; and this he has demonstrated through His powerful and inspiring life. "The Son of Man came not to be served to but to serve and to give his life a ransom for many" (Mark 10:45)— that was his slogan.

The admonitions of Paul and Peter, such as "Let each one of you count others better than yourself" and "he has left for us an example", were emulated as the continuation of the philosophical and practical application of and pointers to what Jesus had taught His disciples (Php. 2, 3; 1 Pet. 2:21).

The dictionary defines 'service' as "the action of helping or doing work for someone." I think service is something more than that. Service is the soul of life. Without service, we cannot truly live. Albert Einstein once said, "Only a life lived for others is a life worthwhile." Only through service can we truly live to our fullest potential. But what does it take to really live? The answer could be, 'one must serve.' This is so profoundly and meaningfully reflected in the lesson of the servant mentioned in Luke chapter 17: "I have only done what is required, *my duty.*"

We can serve in many ways. One can serve by listening, by accumulating treasures of the heart, by awakening people to their fullest potential, by understanding others, by caring for them and so on. In short, to serve is to give. There is no place for ego in a true and honest life. It automatically gets turned off, and one begins to live and love.

What kind of attitudes does the servant have and what are the expressions of this kind of service? It can be simply put in the following way: faithfully manage and handle position and authority; forsaking even the normal and due rights and privileges; no expectation of comforts, dignity and honour; not using influence for ulterior ends; never seeking acceptance, reputation, position and power; respecting others and helping them grow in confidence. These are the fundamental inner dispositions and servant-attitudes that existing and emerging leaders must have. Such individuals have no complain when loss, dishonor, misunderstanding, disaster, adversity, tragedy and failure come their way, because such servants do not have any regard for personal gain; it is only their obligation and duty (Luke 17:10). This state of mind and heart can be reconstituted only through a deep and genuine spiritual transformation—an 'inside out' transformation. A leader—particularly a Christian leader—is one who has been called to serve God and His children.

The leader for tomorrow believes in true leadership, which is all about trying to know and understand the other person sympathetically and empathetically—taking a look at another person's life by giving less attention to personal problems, comforting and developing co-workers and working diligently.

Conclusion

In one of my early ministry situations, we led a lifestyle that we called "fellowship." It can be understood as *koinonia*. We knew that even small things can affect the life, health and activities of a team or a guild. A small misunderstanding, disagreement, unwise conversation and words and small mistakes can hamper relationships and stability. Failure to handle small things can cause big divisions leading to disaster. "Fellowship" united us and acted as a safeguard against disharmony and divisions. It was about sharing and maintaining transparency amongst us even when we harboured unhealthy feelings for someone in our midst.

It may be mentioned that the key to fellowship is open sharing, forgiveness, praying together, solving problems and removing misunderstandings constructively and establishing and maintaining relationships. That was how we kept our team healthy, and work progressed without any hindrances. This is exactly what our Lord Jesus Christ wants us to do. He said "If you come with your gifts to the altar and you feel your brother has anything against you, leave your sacrifice, go and get reconciled with him and then bring your gifts to the altar" (Matt. 5:23-24). This command of the Lord is the foundation stone of this "fellowship." Christian leaders must embrace this command and strive hard to nourish personal relationships and team spirit amongst people.

We must find time to create opportunities for developing open and transparent communication and strong relationships; willingness to forgive and seek forgiveness and praying together are the very fabric of spirituality and leadership empowerment.

Creative and sustainable leadership is the need of the hour. The vision and values of today's leaders are the most important factors in shaping tomorrow's leadership—leaders who would play a significant role in turning the Church into an agent of solace and succour for many.

Listed below are the values that existing leaders must have and that they must try to instil in emerging leaders—the leaders of tomorrow. Today's leaders can use this list on a regular basis to examine their own strengths and weaknesses.

- Seize the opportunities that come around.
- Appreciate every opportunity and situation.
- Make no excuses for not doing.
- Does not pass on blame and excuses to another.
- Own your responsibilities.
- Respect peer group members and collegiums.
- Submit to existing and older leaders.
- Never question the intent if given an assignment.
- Do more than assigned and happily do those your assignment.
- Always complete a project before the deadline.
- Be honest and open to receive corrections and reprimands.
- Always be open to accept failures and mistakes.
- Work hard.
- Make reading a habit.
- Grow consistently and measurably.
- Critique self.
- Be sympathetic to others, not to self.
- Observe closely and learn.
- Ask yourself genuine questions and learn.
- Evaluate consistently.
- Dignity of others should be your top priority.
- Apply new, simple and hard lessons to life.

- Adapt your thinking to the immediate and current context.
- Cultivate performance-oriented attitude and learn from *your successes* and *failures*.
- Never glorify your achievements or past accomplishments.
- Be a team person.
- Keep your deadlines.
- Maintain a things-to-do list and diary.
- Never procrastinate and do not leave things undone.
- Prioritise areas of your life, work and needs.
- Report faithfully.
- Be accountable.
- Keep godly foundations sure and strengthened.
- Be devoted.
- Be positive—always see the good side of everything.
- Be systematic and orderly.
- Keep your working place, especially your working table, neat, clean and orderly.
- Say warm wishes to all before leaving your office.
- Do your assigned work without fail.
- Loyalty should be part of the lifestyle you lead.
- Keep your body fit and healthy.
- Do some physical exercise every day.
- Remain uncompromisingly committed to personal meditation and prayer.
- Smile as much as you can. Wish a warm good morning to those whom you meet.
- Respect everyone.
- Be kind to others.
- Make your bed every day.
- Keep your bathroom neat and clean.

- Be a people person.
- Sleep well; do not oversleep.
- Have good secular and public awareness.
- Be punctual and do not waste your time.
- Put your trust in God. God must be first in life.
- Prioritize work and life.
- People first, then, work.
- Give credit always to others.
- Appreciate every one in the team for the efforts and success.
- Inculcate a positive attitude into everything and for everybody.
- Be constructive in all evaluations and critiquing.
- Never use positions and powers for maintaining power and titles.
- Always look at the broad spectrum of things, then, narrow down perspectives.

The Lord wants to work in his world through you; He wants you to become a true servant-leader. May God of all grace and wisdom help you to become His voice and an instrument of peace in a troubled world. May God bless you!

Endnotes

[1] Michael Green, *Evangelism in the Early Church*, Grand Rapids: W. B. Eerdmans Co., 1970, p. 181.

[2] Leory Eims, *Be a Motivational Leader*, Illinois: Victor Books, 1981, p.55.

[3] *Ibid.*, pp. 56, 57.

[4] Peter C. Wagner, *Your Spiritual Gifts can help Your Church Grow*, Ventura: Regal Books, 1979, p. 49.

A Prayer

O Lord, help me have the mindset of a servant and not to take credit for doing Your work. I am an unworthy servant trying to do my duty towards You. Make me, O God, a servant-leader who understands those who come to me and may You give them the vision and wisdom that would inspire them to follow the gentle Spirit.

Almighty and loving God, open my heart so that I may be sympathetic and nonjudgmental and learn from those who are different from me. Ever-loving God, give me the vision to be humble and meek as You are; and grow in love, gentleness, kindness, mercy and forgiveness. Help me in finding out where my leadership truly lies. Teach me to become a true leader in Your light—a leader who upholds the continuation and extension of Your Son in the world. Teach me to give more importance to Your work than to my personal goals and dreams. And, may I find grace from You to lead those whom You entrust to my care with a heart of humility, gentleness, purity; and ultimately lead them on to You, Amen.

Bibliography

Allan, Roland, *Missionary Methods: St. Pauls or Ours?*, Grand Rapids: W.B. Eerdmans Publishing Co., 1962

Barclay, William, *The Mind of St. Paul*, New York : Harper & Row Publishers, 1958

Blank, Sheldon H., *Understanding the Prophet*, New York: Union of American Hebrew Congregation, 1969.

Bornkamm, Gunther, *Paul* (Translated by D.M.G.Stolker), New York: Harper & Row Publishers, 1971.

Bruce, Alexander Balmain, *The Training of the Twelve*, New Canaan: Keats Publishing Inc., 1979.

Chandapilla, P.T., *Leadership*, Unpublished Article for the Private Circulation among the OM Workers.

Clinton, Robert J., *The Making of a Leader*, Colorado Springs : Navpress, 1988.

Coleman, Robert E., *The Master Plan of Evangelism*, New Jersey: Fleming H. Revell Co., 1963.

Covey, Stephen R., *Principle Centered Leadership*, New York: Simon & Schusher, 1990.

Covey, Stephen R., Seven Habits of Highly Effective People, Free Press, 1989.

Downey, Raymur James, *Old Testament Patterns of Leadership Training: Prophets, Priests and Kings*, Pasadena: M.Th Thesis, Fuller Theological Seminary, 1981.

Eims, Leory, *Be a Motivational Leader*, Illinois: Victor Books, 1981.

Ellis, Joe S., *The Church on Purpose – Keys to Effective Church Leadership, Ohio*: Standard Publishing, 1982.

Bibliography 125

Elliston, Edgar J., *Home Grown Leaders*, Pasadena: Unpublished Draft.

Engstrom, Ted E., *The Making of a Christian Leader*, Grand Rapids: Zondervan Publishing House, 1976.

Erwin, Gayle D., *Jesus Style*, Gospel for Asia Publications, Tiruvalla, 2003.

Gaeblain, Frank E., (Ed), *The Expositors Bible Commentary*, Grand Rapids: Zondervan Publishing House, 1976.

Gangel, Kenneth O., *Building Leadership for Church Education*, Chicago: Moody Press, 1970.

Gibbs, Eddie, *I Believers in Church Growth*, London: Hodder & Stoughton, 1985.

Gilliland, Dean, S., *Pauline Theology and Mission Practice*, Grand Rapids: Baker House, 1983.

Glasser, Arthur F., *Biblical Theology of Mission Practice*, Grand Rapids: Backer Book House, 1983.

Grassi, Joseph A., *A World to Win. The Missionary of Paul the Apostle*, Maryknoll N.Y.: Maryknoll Publications, 1965.

Green, Michael, *Evangelism in the Early Church*, Grand Rapids: W.B. Eerdmans Co., 1970.

Greenslade, Philip, *Leadership, Greatness & Servanthood*, Minneapolis: Bethany House Publishers, 1984.

Hanson, Anthony, T., *The Church of the Servant*, London: S.C.M. Press Ltd., 1962.

Hay, Alexander, *The New Testament Order for Church and Missionary*, Buenos Aires: N.T. Missionary Union.

Hain, Chua Wee, *The Making of a Christian Leader*, Downers Grove: Inter Varsity Press, 1987.

Hooker, Morna Dorothy, *Jesus and the Servant*, London: S.P.C.K., 1959.

Hunter, Archibald M., *The Work and Words of Jesus*, Philadelphia: The Westminster Press, 1950.

Kirkpatrick, John William, *A Theology of Servant Leadership*, Pasadena: D. Miss Dissertation, Fuller Theological Seminary, 1988.

Knight, George. A.F., *Isaiah 40-55, Servant Theology*, Grant Rapids: W.B. Eerdmans Co., 1984.

Knox, John, *Chapters in the life of Paul*, New York: Abingdon, 1950.

Kruse, Colon G., *New Testament Models of Ministry: Jesus & Paul*, Nashville: Thomas Nelson Publishers, 1983.

Ladd, George Eldon, *The Gospel of the Kingdom*, Grand Rapids: W.B. Eerdmans Co., 1986.

Leigh, Ronald W., *Effective Christian Ministry*, Wheaton: Tyndale House Publishers, 1984.

Lenski, R.C. H., *The Interpretation of First and Second Corinthians*, Minnesota Augsburg Publishing House, 1963.

Lindblom, Johannes, *Prophecy in Ancient Israel*, Philadelphia: Muhlenberg Press, 1962.

Maxwell, John, C., *Developing the Leader within You*, Nashville: Thomas Nelson Publishers, 1993.

Manson, T.W., *The Teaching of Jesus: Studies of Form and Context*, Cambridge: University Press, 1951.

Martin, Alfred, *Isaiah – The Salvation of Jehovah*, Chicago: Moody Press, 1956.

Moule, Handley C.G., *The Second Epistle to the Corinthians*, Chicago: Moody Press, 1962.

North, Christopher Richard, *The Suffering Servant in Deutero-Isaiah*, London: Oxford University Press, 1984.

Richards, Lawrence O & Clybe Hoeldtke, *A Theology of Church Leadership*, Grand Rapids: Zondervan Publishing House, 1980.

Richard, Lawrence O., *A Theology of Christian Education*, Grand Rapids: Zondervan Publishing House, 1975.

Ridderbos, Herman, *Paul: An Outline of his Theology*, Grand Rapids: W.B. Eerdmans, 1975.

Ritchie, William, *Life for God Exemplified in the Character and Work of Nehemiah*, London: Adams & Co., 1961.

Robinson, Wheeler H., *The Cross in the Old Testament*, Philadelphia: The Westminster Press, 1955.

Sanders, John Oswald, *Spiritual Leadership*, Chicago: Moody Press, 1980.

Schaeffer, Francis, *Joshua and the Flow of Biblical Ministry*, Downers Grover: Inter Varsity Press, 1975.

Scott, Charles Anderson, *Christianity According to St. Paul*, Cambridge: University Press, 1927.

Snyder, Howard A., *The Community of the King*, Downers Grove: Inter Varsity Press, 1927.

Snyder, Howard A., *Liberating the Church*, Downers Grove: Inter Varsity Press, 1983,

Wagner, Peter C., *Your Spiritual Gifts can help Your Church Grow*, Ventura: Regal Books, 1979.

Watson, David, *I Believe in the Church*, Grand Rapids: W.B. Eerdmans Co., 1978.

Wood, Leon James, *The Prophet of Israel*, Grand Rapids: Baker Book House, 1979.

Wright, Walter C, Relational Leadership, Paternoster, 2002

Yohannan K.P., *The Road to Reality*, Altamonte Springs: Creation House, 1988.

Young, Edward J., *My Servants, The Prophets*, Grand Rapids: W.B. Eerdmans Co., 1952.

Youssef, Michael, *The Leadership Style of Jesus*, Wheaton: Victor Books, 1986.

www.ingramcontent.com/pod-product-compliance
Lightning Source LLC
Chambersburg PA
CBHW032126090426
42743CB00007B/481